We Follow Jesus

Cecilia Crowley
Marie Fursman
Elise Harasyn
Nancy Langhoff
Marie Nachtsheim

Educational and Theological Advisors

Rev. Richard M. Hogan
Rev. John M. LeVoir
Mary Jo Smith

IMAGE OF GOD SERIES

Image of God, Inc., Brooklyn Center, MN 55430

Ignatius Press, San Francisco

Nihil obstat: Mark B. Dosh
                    Censor Librorum

Imprimatur: † John R. Roach, D.D.
                    Archbishop of St. Paul and Minneapolis
                    February 14, 1992

Cover art: Barbara Harasyn

Illustrations: Barbara Harasyn

For additional information about the Image of God program, call 1-800-635-3827

Published 1992 by Ignatius Press, San Francisco
© 1992 Image of God, Inc.
All rights reserved
ISBN 0-89870-332-8
Printed in Hong Kong

Contents

I   God Created Everything

   1   *We Believe in One God*   3

   2   *Angels Are Created*   10

   3   *The Universe Is Created*   15

   4   *People Are Created*   22

II   God Always Loves Us

   5   *Original Sin and Us*   33

   6   *God's Merciful Love*   42

III   Jesus, Our Example

   7   *Jesus' Loving Example*   55

   8   *Jesus Teaches Us the Truth*   61

   9   *Jesus, the King, Rules with Love*   68

  10   *We Help Each Other*   76

  11   *Finding Happiness in Life*   89

IV   Jesus Is with Us

  12   *The Church Guides Us*   103

  13   *With the Help of God's Grace*   120

  14   *We Receive Grace in the Sacraments*   128

V   Acting As an Image of God

  15   *The Ten Commandments*   147

  16   *Loving God*   155

  17   *Loving Others*   159

  18   *We Pray*   174

  19   *Mary, the Mother of God*   182

VI   Liturgical Seasons

  20   *Advent: Preparing for Jesus' Birthday*   205

  21   *Lent: The Path to New Life*   212

Prayers to Know   221

Unit 1

God Created Everything

1

We Believe in One God

What do we call the three Persons in one God?
The Holy Trinity.

Theological . . . studies offer the opportunity for a deeper knowledge of the Person of Christ. But this deeper knowledge does not depend only on our intellectual efforts. It is above all a gift of the Father who, through the Holy Spirit, allows us to know the Son. A person must be 'conformed to Christ' and not merely educated in the faith.

POPE JOHN PAUL II

Vocabulary

person: someone who has a mind and a will.

human person: someone who is created in the image of God with a mind, a will, and a body.

mystery of faith: a truth revealed by God that cannot be fully understood by the human mind.

faith: the power that God gives us that helps us believe what He reveals.

theology: the study of God using the Sacred Scriptures, the teachings of the Church, and reason.

One man who studied about God and taught and wrote about the Holy Trinity was Saint Thomas Aquinas. Thomas was a priest. He is known today as a Doctor of the Church. This means that he was one of the greatest teachers of the Church. Read the following story about Saint Thomas Aquinas.

Saint Thomas Aquinas

THOMAS AQUINAS was born in 1225. He was born of wealthy parents in the family castle in the town of Aquino, Italy. Thomas' parents were members of the nobility.

Although Thomas had a strong and sturdy body, like his father and six older brothers, he did not become a soldier as they had. Instead, Thomas was drawn to the religious life. Thomas was a very quiet boy. He was intelligent and inquisitive, always asking questions.

When Thomas was five years old, he went to live with the Benedictine monks at the Abbey of Monte Cassino. There he studied about God and learned about the religious life. He even wore a Benedictine habit. This didn't mean that he had to become a Benedictine monk, though that was what everyone expected.

When Thomas was fourteen years old, he returned home. A little later, he went to study at the University of Naples (Italy). While in Naples Thomas joined the Dominican Order, whose friars lived a life of poverty. Thomas' family greatly disapproved of this decision. They looked upon the Dominican friars with contempt. They had agreed to a religious life for Thomas if he went to the Benedictine Abbey of Monte Cassino, where most students came from wealthy and noble families. As a monk at the Abbey, backed by his family's influence, Thomas might become a bishop or even a pope. Thomas' family tried various measures to get him to change his mind and become a Benedictine. When even bribery didn't work, Thomas' family had him kidnapped and brought home. They locked Thomas in a tower of one of their castles for about seventeen months. They intended to keep him locked up until he changed his mind. But Thomas did not change his mind. Thomas didn't want the riches offered to him. He had promised to live in poverty. Finally, Thomas' family permitted him to return to the Dominican Order. Thomas made his way to Paris and there learned theology, philosophy, and science from Saint Albert the Great.

Thomas was a large man, and he was quiet and reserved. On first meeting him, fellow students thought Thomas was uninteresting and stupid, because of his size and quiet nature. They soon discovered, however, that Thomas was extremely intelligent, even a genius. He was a very mild and humble man and had an even temper. He did not show off and was always courteous, even when he strongly disagreed with someone. Albert the Great knew that Thomas would be a great teacher one day. Thomas was greatly inspired by Albert and eventually became an even greater teacher than Albert himself.

Thomas became a professor of theology. He spent his life teaching, writing books, meditating, and praying. Thomas would always pray before writing or teaching. His writings and teachings were brilliant and clear. In addition to writing books, Thomas wrote prayers. Once he wrote prayers to be said at the Mass on the feast of Corpus Christi. Saint Bonaventure had also composed Mass prayers for the same feast day. Both Thomas and Bonaventure were to read their prayers to the Pope and cardinals. The Pope and cardinals would then decide which man's prayers would be said at Mass. First, Thomas read the Mass prayers he had composed. Saint Bonaventure listened to Thomas' composition. He knew that the Mass prayers Thomas had composed were much better than his own. Without waiting for the Pope and the cardinals to decide which prayers to use, Saint Bonaventure quietly tore up his own composition.

When Thomas wrote his manuscripts, he dictated to several secretaries at the same time, in order to speed up the writing process. Though the writing was done at top speed, great care was used in making corrections.

The most famous of Thomas' writings is his *Summa theologiae*, which is his summary of Catholic theology. His study of God is divided into three parts: God, creation, and Christ. In his study Thomas used arguments both for and against a particular point. Then he gave a final and convincing argument that proved the truth he was seeking. The *Summa theologiae* is used in seminaries today throughout the world.

Thomas felt that what he had written was but straw, compared with the things God had revealed to him. Toward the end of his life, as Thomas knelt before a crucifix, he heard a voice from the crucifix say, "You have written well of Me, Thomas. What would you have as a reward?" Thomas replied, "Only Yourself, Lord."

Thomas died on March 7, 1274, near Terracina, Italy. Thomas was declared a saint in 1323. He is the patron saint of Catholic schools. His feast day is January 28.

The Holy Trinity

Saint Thomas Aquinas used the Sacred Scriptures (the Bible), the teachings of the Church, and reason in his study of the Holy Trinity. We can do the same.

Using the Sacred Scriptures (the Bible), we can read about the three Persons of the Holy Trinity. Here are two examples of Jesus teaching us about the Holy Trinity. In the first example, Jesus talks about God the Father. Jesus is God the Son. In the second example, Jesus talks about God the Holy Spirit.

Jesus said to him [Thomas the Apostle], "I am the way and the truth and the life. No one comes to the Father except through me. If you know me, then you will also know my Father. From now on you do know him and have seen him." Philip said to him, "Master, show us the Father, and that will be enough for us." Jesus said to him, "Have I been with you for so long a time and you still do not know me, Philip? Whoever has seen me has seen the Father. How can you say, 'Show us the Father?' Do you not believe that I am in the Father and the Father is in me? The words that I speak to you I do not speak on my own. The Father who dwells in me is doing his works. Believe me that I am in the Father and the Father is in me, or else, believe because of the works themselves."
—John 14:6–11

"The Advocate, the holy Spirit that the Father will send in my name—he will teach you everything and remind you of all that [I] told you."
—John 14:26

In the teachings of the Church we have the prayer called the "Apostles' Creed". In the "Apostles' Creed" we state what we believe as Catholics.

Apostles' Creed

I believe in God, the Father almighty,
   creator of heaven and earth.

I believe in Jesus Christ, his only Son, our Lord.
     He was conceived by the power of the Holy Spirit
       and born of the Virgin Mary.
     He suffered under Pontius Pilate,
       was crucified, died, and was buried.
     He descended to the dead.
     On the third day he rose again.
     He ascended into heaven,
       and is seated at the right hand of the Father.
     He will come again to judge the living and the dead.

I believe in the Holy Spirit,
     the holy catholic Church,
     the communion of saints,
     the forgiveness of sins,
     the resurrection of the body,
     and the life everlasting. Amen.

We can see from the Apostles' Creed that the Church teaches us about the Holy Trinity. The Church teaches us about God the Father almighty, about Jesus Christ, His only Son, and about the Holy Spirit.

Using reason, we can try to understand the mystery of the Holy Trinity by looking at our families. Think about your family. How many families live in your house? Usually one family lives in a house. How many people live in your house? Usually one family includes several people. Those people are all separate people, but there is still only one family. In God there are three Persons, but there is still only one God. This example does not come close to explaining the Holy Trinity, but it does offer a small comparison to help us understand the Trinity.

What do we know about each Person in the Holy Trinity? We know that each Person of the Holy Trinity is God. God the Father is God, God the Son is God, and God the Holy Spirit is God. We also know that God is powerful, wise, and loving. He is powerful, because He created everything

from nothing. He is wise, because He knows everything. He is loving, because He loves us and helps us to make loving choices. Each Person of the Holy Trinity is powerful, wise, and loving. One Person is not greater than the other. Even though each Person of the Trinity is powerful, wise, and loving, sometimes we associate power with God the Father, wisdom with God the Son, and love with God the Holy Spirit.

We associate power with God the Father when we say that God the Father created the angels, us, the world, and everything in the world.

We associate wisdom with Jesus, God the Son, when we say that God the Son knows everything. We sometimes call Jesus the Word of God. Jesus teaches us the truth about God. (Of course, Jesus, by His death on the Cross, saved us from sin.)

We associate love with the Holy Spirit when we say that the Holy Spirit is loving. The Holy Spirit guides the Church, and He guides us. He helps us to make loving choices and helps us to follow Jesus.

Though we sometimes associate creating with the Father, teaching with the Son, and loving with the Holy Spirit, it is important to remember that the three Persons of the Trinity always act together—they are *one* God.

We believe in the mystery of the Holy Trinity because Jesus, God the Son, taught us this truth. We also believe because God has given us the gift of faith. Faith is the power that God gives us that helps us believe what He reveals.

There is a story told about Saint Augustine of Hippo. Saint Augustine lived many, many years ago. He studied about God and the Holy Trinity. One day, he was walking along the seashore thinking about the mystery of the Holy Trinity. Saint Augustine saw a small boy digging a hole in the sand. Then the boy began filling the hole with sea water. He filled a shell with water from the ocean and emptied the water into the hole he had dug.

Saint Augustine asked the boy what he was doing. The boy explained that he was trying to empty the ocean into the little hole he had dug.

Saint Augustine told the boy that he could not possibly empty the enormous ocean into such a small hole. The boy replied that it would be easier for him to put all the water from the ocean into the little hole than it would be for Saint Augustine to understand the mystery of the Trinity. After the boy said this, he vanished. The boy was really an angel.

The angel was telling Saint Augustine that the human mind doesn't have the ability to understand God completely, because He is Divine. The Holy Trinity is one of the mysteries of faith that we cannot completely understand.

Even though we cannot completely understand God, we should continue to learn as much as we can about Him. We should pay attention in religion class, and we should do our religion homework.

We should go to Mass on Sundays and Holy Days. On one particular Sunday, the Church especially worships the Holy Trinity. That Sunday is called Trinity Sunday. It is the first Sunday after Pentecost. On that Sunday we pray: "We joyfully proclaim our faith in the mystery of your Godhead. . . . three Persons equal in majesty, undivided in splendor, yet one Lord, one God, ever to be adored in your everlasting glory."

We should also pray each day, thanking God for His gifts to us and asking God to help us follow Him always. When we make the Sign of the Cross, we are praising the Holy Trinity and showing that we believe that in one God there are three Persons.

The "Glory Be" reminds us that each Person of the Holy Trinity always was, is now, and always will be.

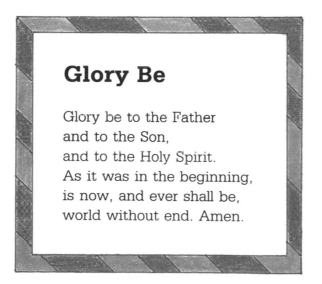

Glory Be

Glory be to the Father
and to the Son,
and to the Holy Spirit.
As it was in the beginning,
is now, and ever shall be,
world without end. Amen.

2

Angels Are Created

Who are angels?

Angels are images of God. They are persons created by God without bodies. They are pure spirits with minds and wills.

What gift did God give the angels?

God created the angels in His image with the gift of His life, which is grace.

Where are the angels who love God and are faithful to Him?

They are in heaven praising and worshiping God.

Where are the angels who do not love God and are unfaithful to Him?

They have separated themselves from God and are in a place created for them, called hell.

For to his angels he has given command about you, that they guard you in all your ways.   PSALM 91:11

Vocabulary

create: to make something from nothing. Only God can create.

angels: images of God, persons created by God without bodies. They are pure spirits with minds and wills.

devils: unfaithful angels who chose not to act as images of God.

heaven: a place of perfect happiness, where there is love of God, love of neighbor, and love of self.

hell: a place of eternal separation from God, where there is no love of God, no love of neighbor, and no love of self.

eternal: always was, always is, and always will be.

pure spirits: persons with minds and wills but no bodies.

What Angels Are

God created the angels in His image. As images of God, angels are persons. They have minds to think and wills to choose. The angels are pure spirits, that is, they were created without bodies. We cannot see angels. God created the angels to know Him and to love Him. As pure spirits, angels are more like God than human persons. They are wiser and more powerful than human persons. They know more about God than we do here on earth. Any choice or decision an angel makes is made with full knowledge. Angels do not change their minds.

The angels were blessed from their creation with grace, God's life. Grace is all the angels will ever need to live with God in heaven. They were created by God in His image to love and worship Him forever. With all of this, how could some of the angels choose not to love God? It was possible for them to choose not to love God, because the angels have free wills. God created the angels free, so that they could freely choose to love. As images of God, they were created to love. But, if God forced the angels to love Him, that wouldn't really be love; it would be force. Love is always freely chosen. God gave the angels freedom, so that their love could be freely chosen. Some angels, led by Satan, chose not to love God. We call these angels the unfaithful angels, or devils.

Work the puzzle below and find the coded message. Use the codes to find out what letter each symbol stands for.

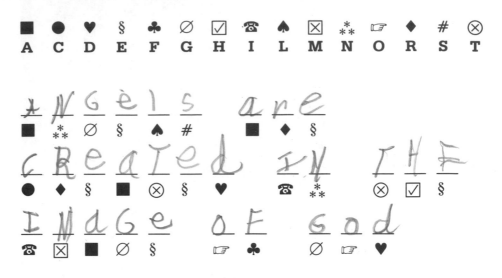

■	●	♥	§	♣	∅	☑	☎	♠	⊠	⁑	☞	◆	#	⊗
A	C	D	E	F	G	H	I	L	M	N	O	R	S	T

ANGELS
■ ⁑ ∅ § ♠ #   ■ ◆ §

CREATED IN THE
● ◆ § ■ ⊗ § ♥   ☎ ⁑   ⊗ ☑ §

IMAGE OF GOD
☎ ⊠ ■ ∅ §   ☞ ♣   ∅ ☞ ♥

A STORY OF FAITH

Saint Michael the Archangel

GOD created the angels in His image. He created them to love Him as He loved them. The angels were very happy loving and praising God. Among them were some very powerful angels called archangels. The names of some of the archangels are Gabriel, Raphael, and Michael. These angels are very strong and special friends of God.

One of the angels, named Lucifer, decided that he didn't want to love God. He wanted to be just as important and powerful as God. Lucifer led a group of angels who also were too proud to love God. They wanted to be gods. (Today we call Lucifer Satan.)

Saint Michael the Archangel and the other faithful angels struggled with Lucifer and the other unfaithful angels. Lucifer and the unfaithful angels no longer chose to live with God. They no longer wanted God's life, grace. They chose a place created for them called hell.

The Faithful Angels

When Satan and some of the other angels turned away from God, they turned away from all that is good, from all that is true, and from all that is love. They chose not to act as images of God. They chose to live an existence apart from God, where there is no love of God, no love of neighbor, and no love of self. They used their freedom to choose what we call hell. Through their free choice, evil happened.

Satan and his followers can tempt us to turn away from God. However, they cannot make us sin. All persons can freely choose to respond to God's love. By responding to God's love we become the best images of God we can be. When we are tempted to do something wrong, we can pray to Saint Michael and the other faithful angels, who will help us act as images of God.

The angels who chose to love God and to be faithful to Him remained with God in heaven and help us in our relationships with God and others. These angels praise God eternally on behalf of all the created world. Some of the angels are sent by God to us as messengers. Some are guardian angels, who are sent to us to help us and sometimes to protect us from evil. At times, these angels may influence us to do good things. We can pray and ask our guardian angels to bring our prayers to God.

Answer the following questions in your own words.

1 Why did some of the angels choose not to love God and be faithful to Him?

_____

_____

_____

2 Where are the angels who chose not to love God?

_____

_____

3 Where are the angels who chose to love God?

_____

_____

4 Angels have minds and wills. What does this mean?

_____

_____

Fill in the blanks below, and then find the answers in the Word Search following the statements. These are some of the words you will use.

hell	God	devils	grace
heaven	create	angels	

1 We call _____ a place of perfect happiness, where there is love of God, love of neighbor, and love of self.

2 To _____ is to make something from nothing.

3 We call _____ the place of eternal separation from God, where there is no love of God, no love of neighbor, and no love of self.

4 _____ are images of God created by God without bodies. They are pure spirits with minds and wills.

5 The _____ are the angels who chose not to act as images of God.

6 _____ is the gift of God's life that He gave the angels and us.

7 Persons, both angels and humans, are made in the image of _____.

```
D  E  F  L  M  S  T  O  W  L  J  R
N  P  C  R  E  A  T  E  L  H  L  V
D  O  E  P  I  K  M  J  F  A  E  U
E  S  G  A  H  E  A  V  E  N  Z  B
V  T  O  D  E  H  R  Q  N  G  F  J
I  A  D  R  L  S  C  V  B  E  N  C
L  D  O  U  L  Z  G  W  F  L  O  W
S  R  G  R  A  C  E  T  P  S  M  S
```

3

The Universe Is Created

Why did God create everything?
To share His goodness and love.

May all creation give glory and praise to you, O LORD.
I will sing praise to you, my God, all my life.
Bless the LORD, O my soul!

BASED ON PSALM 104

The Story of Creation

In the beginning, there was only God. Then, because of His goodness and love, God made everything from nothing.

God made the angels to share heaven with Him. The angels are persons with minds to think and wills to make choices. The angels are pure spirits; they do not have bodies.

When God created the heavens and the earth, the earth was a barren land covered with water, and darkness was everywhere.

Then God said, "Let there be light", and there was light. God saw how good the light was. God separated the light from the darkness. He called the light "day" and the darkness "night".

God made the blue sky. He gathered some of the water to be the great oceans. Some of the water He gathered into fresh-water lakes and streams. God made the dry land to appear, and He called the dry land "the earth".

Then God said, "Let the earth bring forth vegetation: every kind of plant that bears seed and every kind of fruit tree on earth that bears fruit with its seed in it." So it happened. God covered the earth with all kinds of plants and many trees of various shapes and sizes, including the trees with fruit. The earth was full of color and beautiful to look at.

Then God made two great lights in the sky to separate the day from the night. The greater light, the sun, He made to shine during the day. The lesser light, the moon, He made to shine at night. He also made the stars to shine at night.

Then God filled the waters with whales, fish, and many different swimming creatures. God made all kinds of birds to fly in the skies. God saw how good it was, and He blessed them.

Then God said, "Let the earth bring forth all kinds of living creatures: cattle, creeping things, and wild animals of all kinds." So it happened. God made all the animals of the earth.

Then God said: "Let us make man in our image, after our likeness." God created man in His image; in the divine image He created him; male and female He created them.

So it was that God created the first man, Adam, and the first woman, Eve. Adam and Eve were different from the rest of God's creations. Only Adam and Eve were persons with bodies—created in the image of God with minds and wills.

God gave to Adam and Eve the care of the wonderful world He had made and everything in it.

When God completed all His work of creation, He rested. He looked at all He had made and saw it was very good.

God did not have to create the angels, human beings, or the world. God freely chose to create all things to share His goodness and love.

—based on Genesis 1:1–31 and 2:1–2

When God created the world, everything was beautiful and balanced. Everything had a proper place or was in a proper order. God gave people the responsibility of taking care of all His gifts.

Praise the Lord for His Creation

Bless the LORD, O my soul!
O LORD, my God, you are great and wonderful.
All majesty and glory are yours.

Out of your love
you created the heavens and the earth.
In the wide blue sky,
you made the sun to shine by day,
giving light and warmth.
As evening comes, the moon and the stars
give light to the darkness.

You made the mountains and the valleys;
and the oceans you set
in a place you had fixed for them.

You made lakes and streams
that wind among the mountains,
giving drink to all living things.
In the waters you put swimming creatures,
both great and small.

You filled the skies with all kinds of birds.
The birds build their nests in the trees you planted,
and from the branches the birds send forth their songs.

How many are your works, O LORD!
The earth is full of your creatures.
In wisdom you have made them all.

You send rain to water the earth,
and the land is plentiful
with the fruits of your works.

You raise grass for the cattle
and vegetation for people's use.
At sunrise people work to gather from the earth
the food and drink that you have promised.

All of your creations depend on you for life,
and you give them all that they need.
In your great love, you send forth your Spirit
and continue your creative work.

With each new day that dawns,
each new flower that blooms,
with each new child that's born,
you renew the face of the earth.

May all creation give glory and praise
to you, O LORD.
I will sing praise to you, my God,
Bless the LORD, O my soul!

BASED ON PSALM 104

The following story describes what might happen if we don't appreciate God's creations and take care of them.

One Strange Dream

ONE day, Adam and Tony were walking home from school. Adam was eating a candy bar. As he took the last bite, he let the wrapper fall to the ground. Tony said, "Hey! You dropped your candy wrapper."

"So, I don't need it anymore," answered Adam.

"Haven't you heard that you shouldn't be a litterbug?"

Adam retorted, "Knock it off! I don't need to be a goodie-two-shoes."

Tony was disappointed. He thought that everyone should help take care of the earth.

That night, Adam did not sleep very well. He kept tossing and turning. Then suddenly he saw two large green creatures with wings. They wrapped him in a sheet and flew off with him.

Adam cried, "Where are you taking me?" But there was no answer.

After what seemed a very long time, the creatures landed. Adam was set free. He looked around. There was the most beautiful sight he had ever seen. There was a lake so clear that he could see tadpoles swimming and shiny rocks on the bottom. He could see the sun reflected in the water and the bluest sky he had ever seen. In the distance, he could see the tops of the mountains. The grass was a bright green that resembled plush carpeting. There were all kinds of animals around. All of the animals had plenty to eat. Beautiful birds flew in the sky.

Adam turned to the two creatures, "Where am I? Who are you? I've never seen any place like this before. Where are all the people?"

The two creatures looked at each other, and then one replied, "My name is Jake and my friend's name is José. This is the planet earth. You do not see any people, because they have not been created yet."

"What?" exclaimed Adam.

José explained, "This is what the world looked like before man was created."

"Why are you showing me all this?" asked Adam.

Jake and José wouldn't give Adam a reason. Jake would only reply, "Take a look around you."

Adam said, "Everything is so clean and healthy looking. Why haven't I been to such a great place before?" Again there was no answer.

Suddenly there was a great wind! Adam felt himself spinning around. He spun so fast he became dizzy and couldn't see. Adam felt as if he were being lifted up and down. Suddenly the spinning stopped, the wind quit, and he found himself sitting on the ground. Adam stood up and looked around.

He was in the same place, but it looked somewhat different. Adam asked, "Why have things changed?"

José answered, "Look around and see if you can notice what is different."

Adam looked toward the mountains. Adam had trouble seeing the tops of the mountains. There seemed to be a haze covering everything. There were no more tadpoles in the lake. He could barely see the pebbles at the bottom. They were no longer shiny, but dull and gray. There weren't as many trees, and the grass had several worn spots. Some of the different kinds of animals had disappeared. Now there were tall shiny buildings, with smoke puffing out of the smoke stacks. A pipe coming out of one of the buildings was draining sludge into the lake. Adam noticed there were people walking around.

Two boys were eating candy bars. They both threw their wrappers on the ground. Adam saw pop cans and fast-food containers on the ground. A boat sped around the lake. Adam could see the gasoline from the old motor dripping into the lake. He wondered how anything could live in the lake.

Adam remembered that he always dropped his wrappers and paper on the ground. He wondered . . .

Suddenly a strong wind blew up. Again, Adam felt himself spinning around. Again he felt dizzy, as if he were going up and down. Abruptly, the spinning stopped.

Adam looked around him. José and Jake were still with him, but Adam thought he was in a new place. "Where is this place?" asked Adam.

"Look around you. We are standing in the same spot, only many years later," replied Jake.

Adam couldn't believe his eyes! There were no trees and no grass. No way could he see any of the mountains! Where was the sun? He thought he saw a hazy spot in the sky that might be the sun. The water had disappeared from the lake. Instead, the lake was filled with thick, oily sludge. The buildings were no longer shiny but were dusty, gray, and empty. There were no people around at all! Adam didn't see any animals, birds, or fish. Instead of trees and grass, he saw piles of garbage decorating the land.

Adam picked up one of the rusty cans. He turned toward José and Jake and asked, "Where are all the people and the animals?"

José answered with a question, "What are some of the things people need in order to live?"

"Food and water", replied Adam.

Jake replied, "God loves us. He created the world with everything in it. Then he created people. However, humans forgot to take care of His beautiful creations. Plants cannot live without clean air or water; animals can't live without other animals, plants, and water. People need water. People get food from the plants and animals. But people have not taken care of God's creations. This is the result—you see what the earth is like because of neglect."

"How can we change it? Can we save the world?" asked Adam.

José said, "If people don't change their ways, they will destroy all of God's creations. You have just experienced what the world might look like in the future. If you and everyone else will begin to think about the earth and to take care of it, it does not have to end up this way."

Suddenly, a strong wind blew. Again, Adam felt dizzy and felt himself going up and down. When the motion stopped, he found himself in bed. Adam jumped up and looked outside. It was a nice, sunny day, and the sky was clear blue. "Aww . . . it was just a dream! I don't have to worry." Then he saw a rusty pop can. Maybe everything had really happened.

Adam got dressed and ran to the park. He joined his friends at the food stand. After they had purchased their food, the friends walked along the path toward the lake. David dropped the paper sack when he took the food out.

Adam picked up the sack and threw it in a nearby trash can. Adam said, "You should be more careful." David couldn't believe his ears! Adam had never thrown anything away before! David just stood and stared at Adam.

When they reached the lake, Terry flipped the lid to his orange juice into the lake. Joel threw his glass at the ducks that were swimming by.

"What's the matter with you guys? Don't you know we have to take care of our earth? It's the only one we have. If we don't take care of it, we'll lose it", yelled Adam.

"Gee, Adam, you're right. We do need to take care of our earth. I guess we didn't think about it before", said David.

"I've been doing a lot of thinking. All of us have to take care of the earth and all of God's creations. We have to try to get other people to do the same," replied Adam.

"What kinds of things can we do?" asked Joel.

In Your Own Words

Think of five ways that you can help take care of God's creations.

1 _____

2 _____

3 _____

4 _____

5 _____

4

People Are Created

Why did God create persons?
God created persons out of a desire to share His goodness and love with them.

•

Why did God allow Adam to experience loneliness?
God allowed Adam to experience loneliness so Adam could discover for himself how unique he was.

Why shouldn't we use other people?
People are made in the image of God. As images of God, they have dignity, and they deserve our respect.

*You have made him little less than the angels
and crowned him with glory and honor.
You have given him rule over the works of your hands,
putting all things under his feet.*

PSALM 8:6-7

Vocabulary

love: to choose freely to give oneself to God and others.
awe: great wonder, together with deep respect.
dominion: being in charge of; having authority or stewardship.

God's Creation
God created the world and everything in it.

*Then God said: "Let us make man in our image, after our likeness.
Let them have dominion over the fish of the sea, the birds of the
air, and the cattle, and over all the wild animals and all the
creatures that crawl on the ground." God created man in his
image; in the divine image he created him; male and female he
created them.*
—Genesis 1:26–27

God created all things and all people. He gave everything to us—the
fields, fruits, sun, rain, animals—everything necessary for us to live. All that
we have is a gift of God's love. When God created the world, He gave
Himself to the world He loved. He created us in His image and likeness to
do what He does. When we do what God does—love—our actions reflect
His actions. We can act like God because we are reflections, or images, of
God. As images of God, we have minds to think and wills to make choices.
Animals cannot think or choose. They can only seek food, life, and
protection for themselves. Animals act in a certain way all the time. They
cannot think, and they cannot choose how to act or what to do. We are able
to think with our minds and to make choices with our wills. What kinds of
choices have you made today? As images of God, we should try to make
right choices.

God created the world and everything in it out of a desire to share His
goodness and love. God created many things on earth that we may use and
enjoy. He gave us land to grow our food, water for us to drink, animals to
help us with our work, and many other things.

The one creation of God's that we may not use is people. People are
made in the image of God. As images of God we have dignity, and we
deserve each other's respect. As images of God we should love God and
others. Sometimes we fail to love and respect others as we should. We fail
when we use people.

FOR DISCUSSION

Read the following stories. In the space provided after each story, answer the question. Then explain your answer.

1 Dan does not like to do his math. It takes him a long time to finish the problems, and he just does not like spending so much time on math. There are so many more interesting things to do. There is a new student, Jack, who is really good at math—and he is really fast! Jack offers to help Dan. Dan finds that he is finishing his math homework in less than half the time with Jack's help. Dan goes to Jack's house every night, so that he can get his math done quickly. When Dan is done with his math, he leaves to have fun with his friends, but he does not ask Jack to come along. In fact, Dan never invites Jack along when he and his friends are going somewhere. Also, Dan hardly talks to Jack in school.

Is Jack being used? _____yes_____

Explain: _Jack is being used because Dan doesn't ask him to play with Dan and his friends._

2 Karen wants to go to her friend's house after supper, but it is Karen's turn to do the dishes. Karen decides to be extra nice to her brother, Dave, and then to ask him to do the dishes for her after supper, so that she can go to her friend's house. Dave agrees to do the dishes for Karen, but Karen does not offer to do the dishes the following night for Dave.

Is Karen using Dave? _____yes_____

Explain: _She was being nice to Dave so he would do dishes for Karen._

3 Susan goes home with Sally after school only when Sally's mom is working late. When Sally's mom works late, she is not there to tell the girls not to eat cookies, drink pop, or watch television. Susan does not want to go home with Sally when Sally's mom is there, because her mom does not allow eating a lot of snacks after school.

Is Susan using Sally? _Yes_

Explain: _Susan just wants to drink pop, watch tv, and eat cookies._

---

4 Bob's friend Tommy wants to come over to Bob's house only when there is a good program on cable TV. Bob does not see Tommy any other time—Tommy does not want to play baseball, ride bikes, and so forth. When Tommy does come to Bob's house, he does not talk very much to Bob, because he is paying so much attention to TV.

Is Bob being used? _Yes_

Explain: _Tommy just wants to watch cable tv._

Truly you have formed my inmost being; you knit me in my mother's womb. I give you thanks that I am fearfully, wonderfully made. . . .
    —Psalm 139:13–14

Different Persons, Different Talents

God created us as unique individuals, with different talents and personalities. No two persons, not even "identical" twins, are exactly alike. There has never been a person exactly like you before, and there will never be one exactly like you in the future.

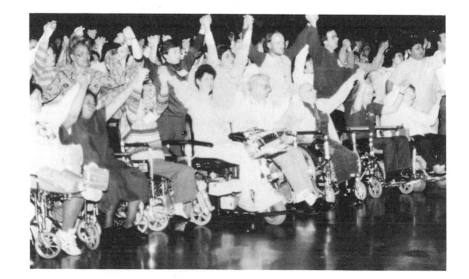

We each have many talents, but we may be better at one thing than at another. We do not all have the same talents. One person's talents are not more important than another's. The important thing is that we use our talents to love others and care for them. Here is the story of one person who used her talents to love others and care for them.

A STORY OF FAITH

Saint Elizabeth of Hungary

During the period of time called the Middle Ages, in the year 1207, Princess Elizabeth was born to King Andrew and Queen Gertrude of Hungary.

It was a time of kings and queens, princes and princesses, knights and castles. The kings and princes ruled over small states and were often at war with one another. The castles were defended by armies of knights. Some of these knights lived in houses around the castle. Many servants worked and lived in these houses and were treated almost as if they were slaves.

Peasants lived in the village and worked hard for their money. The taxes they paid helped to support those who were rich. Beggars came to the castle gates, hoping that one of the ladies or knights would give them a coin or a crust of bread.

Some of the princes and kings made agreements to help defend the others' lands if attacked. King Hermann of Thuringia, a small state in Germany, and King Andrew of Hungary made such an agreement. A marriage was arranged between Princess Elizabeth, King Andrew's daughter, and Louis, King Hermann's son. The marriage was arranged shortly after Elizabeth was born.

When Elizabeth was only four years old, she went to live in the castle of Thuringia. She was a small child with dark hair and a happy, cheerful personality. But she was sad and frightened to be leaving her home and parents and going to live in a strange place with people she did not know. When she arrived at the castle, she met Louis, who was ten years old, and his family. Louis and Elizabeth became good friends and cared for each other.

Louis was being educated in many subject areas, so that he would be prepared for the time when he would be king of Thuringia. He studied languages and math. He learned to swim and how to use the weapons of knighthood. Elizabeth learned to do embroidery, to sing and to play a musical instrument, and to ride a horse. She also learned the things she would need to know as queen of Thuringia.

Elizabeth often spent time in the castle chapel. There she prayed to God and talked to Him about the things that hurt her and made her sad. She prayed each day, she made many small sacrifices, and she was very generous. She gave big baskets of food to the beggars at the castle gates and gave away many of the things that she liked the most. She was also patient and forgiving. Some of the rich ladies in the castle spoke unkindly about Elizabeth, because they did not like all the things she did to show her love for God. Many of the people in the castle did not understand her and wanted her to be sent back to Hungary. Louis would not allow it, however, for he loved and cared for Elizabeth.

At the age of fifteen, when his father died, Louis became King of Thuringia. He had been well trained, and he managed the affairs of the kingdom very well.

When Louis was twenty-one years old, and Elizabeth was fourteen, they were married. Together they ruled Thuringia and were very happy. Over the next few years they had a son, Hermann, and a daughter, Sophia. During this time, they often went to the village, where they spoke with the villagers and listened to their concerns. Elizabeth cleaned the homes of the poor, and she cared for those who were sick. This was difficult for her to do, because she had a dislike for disease and ugliness. She overcame this dislike, however, and even went to the leper colony to bring the lepers food, clothes, and money. She told them about Jesus, Who had died for them.

Elizabeth gave away her beautiful clothes and kept only plain clothes for herself. However, when there were special occasions on which she needed to be dressed like a queen, God always provided her with the most beautiful clothes.

One very cold winter, when Louis was away to see the emperor, there was a famine. The peasants and beggars especially were lacking food. Elizabeth sold her jewels and anything else that she could to raise money to help the poor. She also used the grain from the castle bins and made bread each day, which she gave to the poor and hungry. The people who lived in the castle were very angry, because they were afraid that they would not have enough to eat.

When the worst part of that winter was over, people suddenly became sick with smallpox, and many died. People were afraid they would get the disease if they touched the bodies of the dead, so they would not bury them. Elizabeth asked God to watch over her, and then she went out to care for the sick and bury the dead. When the people saw her doing this, they followed her example and began to help each other. There were so many sick people to be cared for that Elizabeth had a hospital built and trained nurses to care for the people. Finally the sickness was over, and the terrible time came to an end. All the money was gone, and the castle grain was almost gone. When Louis returned home, the rich people complained to him that Elizabeth had given everything away to the poor and that the grain was nearly gone. Louis defended Elizabeth and did not get upset with her. When the people took Louis to show him that the granaries were nearly empty, they found instead that the grain bins were so full the grain was running over the top and onto the floor.

Later, Louis went to war to protect the Holy Land, the land where Jesus had lived. This war was called a crusade. Elizabeth was very sad. She was soon to have another child, and she would miss Louis very much. Elizabeth rode along with Louis and the army until they reached the border of Thuringia. There she and Louis said their good-byes. Elizabeth then went back to the castle and spent much of her time caring for the poor and the sick. Louis and the army continued their journey to the Holy Land. Many of

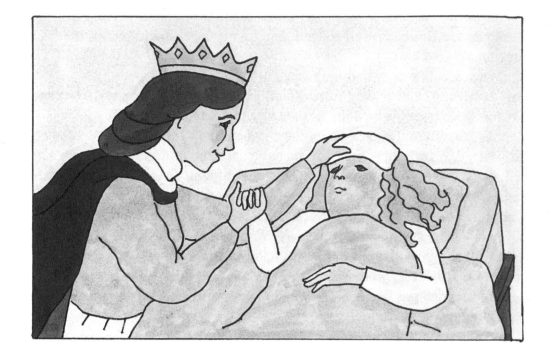

the men became sick with a fever, and some of them died. Louis also became very sick, but he continued the journey until he could go no farther, and, at the age of twenty-seven, Louis died.

Elizabeth heard of Louis' death three weeks later, about the time that their little daughter Gertrude was born. Elizabeth was filled with deep sorrow. She had lost her husband, and, without him to protect her, she was treated cruelly by the people. In addition, Louis' brother, Henry, took over as king, although that role rightfully belonged to Louis' son.

Finally, one cold, dark night, Elizabeth left the castle and took her children with her. A friendly tavernkeeper let them use an old shed that he had used for his pigs. When Elizabeth's aunt, who was the head of a convent, heard of her troubles, she invited Elizabeth and her family to live at the convent with the nuns. Elizabeth and her children lived there until the knights of Louis' army brought his body back to Thuringia. At his funeral, there was a reconciliation between Henry and Elizabeth. Henry acknowledged Louis' son as king of Thuringia, and he provided Elizabeth with money and a place to live. Elizabeth chose to live a life of poverty, in imitation of Saint Francis, and to do works of charity. Elizabeth's son and older daughter were raised at the castle, and her younger daughter was raised by nuns at a convent.

Elizabeth fasted and prayed. She continued her work of caring for the poor, the sick, and the lepers. On November 17, 1231, after becoming very ill with a fever, Elizabeth died. She was twenty-four. Even before she was buried, miracles began to occur. People who were blind regained their sight. Lepers were healed, as well as people who were lame or crippled.

Three and a half years after her death, Elizabeth was declared a saint by Pope Gregory IX. During her short lifetime, Elizabeth had set an example of Christian charity and love for God. Her feast day is November 17.

Saint Elizabeth of Hungary used her talents to love others and care for them. Write down three things that you have learned about Saint Elizabeth of Hungary after reading the story.

- _____

  _____

- _____

  _____

  _____

- _____

  _____

We can imitate Saint Elizabeth of Hungary by using our talents to love others and care for them. What are some of your talents, and how can you use them to love others and care for them?

- _____

  _____

- _____

  _____

- _____

  _____

Fill in the blanks below with the following words and phrases. Use each word or phrase only once.

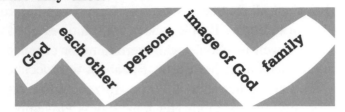

God   each other   persons   image of God   family

1   Only _____ can love and be loved.

2   Adam and Eve chose to love _____ and love _____.

3   Adam and Eve became the first _____.

4   Adam and Eve were created in the _____.

Complete the following exercise in your own words.

1   What is love?

    _____

    _____

2   Why can we think and choose?

    _____

    _____

3   Give an example of how one person might use another person, and explain why it is wrong to do so.

    _____

    _____

    _____

    _____

    _____

    _____

    _____

    _____

Unit 2

God
Always
Loves
Us

5

Original Sin and Us

How did Adam and Eve hurt themselves when they chose to sin?

1. They lost God's gift of grace and were not able to share God's life on earth or live with Him in heaven.
2. They wounded their abilities to think and to choose.
3. They wounded their bodies and would experience suffering and death.

How are we affected by original sin?

1. We are born without grace.
2. Our abilities to think and to choose are wounded.
3. Our bodies will experience suffering and death.

Should not Adam and Eve have been faithful to God? Certainly. And instead they disobeyed, and lost His friendship.

But the Lord loved them, as your parents love each of you. Then He thought of saving them by sending them a Redeemer, that is, Jesus Christ, His Son. He would come, He would teach the way of truth, and then He would die to make up for men's sins. You see, then, God's goodness: . . . He at once promised salvation by means of the Redeemer.

POPE JOHN PAUL II

Vocabulary

original sin: the first sin of Adam and Eve. We inherit original sin from Adam and Eve, which means we are conceived and born without grace.

Adam and Eve and Original Sin

WHEN God created Adam and Eve, He shared His life, grace, with them. He gave them a beautiful place to live, called the Garden of Eden. The garden was filled with beautiful flowers, animals of every kind, fish in the lakes and streams, and birds nesting in the trees. There were many fruit trees, which provided food for Adam and Eve. God gave Adam and Eve that beautiful garden in which to live. God asked only one thing of them. In the center of the garden stood the tree of knowledge of good and evil. God told Adam and Eve that they could eat the fruit of all the trees, except for this tree. If Adam and Eve were to eat the fruit from this tree, they would not be able to live with God forever.

Not eating the fruit of the tree of good and evil seemed like such a little thing, and at first it was easy for Adam and Eve to obey God. They were made in God's image and likeness. Their minds and wills had complete control over their bodies. Adam and Eve listened to God, and they obeyed God. They loved God and were very happy, until one day a serpent came and spoke to Eve. The serpent was really the devil. The devil wanted to spoil everything. He wanted Adam and Eve to disobey God.

The devil asked Eve, "Did God really tell you not to eat from any of the trees in the garden?"

Satan knew that he could not tempt Adam and Eve into eating the fruit by appealing to their sense of taste, or smell, or sight. Their minds had control over their bodies, so Adam and Eve could not be tempted so easily.

Eve told the devil that it was just the fruit of the tree of good and evil that they should not eat. If they ate this fruit, they would not be able to live with God in heaven.

The devil was very clever. He appealed directly to Eve's mind and lied to her, saying, "You certainly will not die! No. God knows well that the moment you eat of it your eyes will be opened, and you will be like gods who know what is good and what is evil."

The devil told Eve that God was jealous and did not want Adam and Eve to have the same powers that He had.

Eve must have known that the devil was lying, but she chose to disobey God. Eve picked a fruit from the tree of good and evil. She ate some of the fruit. Then she gave some of the fruit to Adam and told him to taste it. Eve told Adam the fruit was from the tree of good and evil, and that it would make them as wise as God. Adam took the fruit and ate some of it.

Like the unfaithful angels, Adam and Eve sinned. It was a sin of pride. They had wanted to be as wise and powerful as God. They thought that would make them happy. Adam and Eve chose to disobey God. They chose not to trust Him. Instead of being happy, Adam and Eve felt very ashamed. They knew that they had not loved God as they should, that they had sinned.

Adam and Eve tried to hide from God. But God called to Adam and asked, "Where are you?" Adam answered, "I heard you in the garden; but I was afraid, . . . so I hid myself."

Then God said, "You have eaten, then, from the tree of which I had forbidden you to eat!"

Adam then blamed Eve, saying, "The woman whom you put here with me—she gave me fruit from the tree, and so I ate it."

God then asked Eve, "Why did you do such a thing?"

Eve blamed the devil, saying, "The serpent tricked me into it, so I ate it."

—based on Genesis 3

Original Sin and Its Results

Adam and Eve chose to disobey God. They hurt the relationship they shared with God. This sin of Adam and Eve was the first sin. We call it the "original sin".

After sin, Adam and Eve could no longer live in the Garden of Eden. They had to work very hard for their shelter and food. They would suffer from the cold, and they would get sick. They would experience death.

After sin, it was hard for them to know what was right and to make the right choices. Most important, Adam and Eve lost grace. Adam and Eve were very unhappy.

God still loved Adam and Eve, but the love between God and Adam and Eve was weaker. God gave them clothes made from skins to wear, as a sign that He loved and cared for them.

God promised Adam and Eve that He would send a Savior. The Savior would be for Adam and Eve and their descendants. He would teach people who they are and show them how they should act as images of God. The Savior would return God's love and help them return God's love.

Our parents and guardians make decisions that affect the whole family, for example, where we go to school and where we live. Adam and Eve made a decision that affected them and all of their descendants, except Jesus and Mary. Adam and Eve chose to sin. When Adam and Eve committed the original sin, they lost grace, and they were not able to live with God in heaven. They were not able to love each other as they should. It was hard for them to know what was right and to make the right choices. They could no longer live in the Garden of Eden, and they had to work very hard for their food and shelter. They would suffer and die. Original sin and its effects were passed on to their descendants.

Cain and Abel were sons of Adam and Eve. As descendants of Adam and Eve, Cain and Abel suffered from original sin and its effects. Cain and Abel lacked grace. It was hard for them to know what was right and to make the right choices. They also had to work hard for their food, clothing, and shelter. In the following story we will see original sin and its effects reflected in the choices Cain made.

Cain's Wrong Choice

CAIN AND ABEL were sons of Adam and Eve. God loved Cain and Abel. Abel grew up and became a shepherd, while Cain chose to become a farmer.

Abel wanted to offer a sacrifice to God. He waited for his sheep to have their lambs. Abel wanted these lambs very much. When the lambs were finally born, he offered the firstborn lamb to God as a sacrifice. God was very pleased with Abel and his offering. God accepted Abel's sacrifice.

Cain grew lots of food. Eventually, Cain offered a part of a harvest to God. God was not pleased with this gift. God did not accept Cain's gift. Cain was envious of his brother Abel, because God had accepted Abel's sacrifice and not his. Cain became angry at Abel. Cain thought of a plan to hurt his brother. Cain asked Abel to go into a field with him. When they were in the field, Cain turned on his brother and killed him. God knew what Cain had done. He asked Cain, "Where is your brother Abel?"

Cain answered, "I do not know. Am I my brother's keeper?"

The Lord then said, "What have you done!"

The Lord told Cain he had done a terrible thing to his brother. The Lord also told Cain how he had hurt himself when he killed his brother. As a result, he would no longer be able to farm. He would have to wander far from home. Cain had lost his home and would never be able to find a place to settle down. Cain feared that, as a wanderer, he would soon be murdered. "Not so!", the Lord said to him. The Lord placed a special mark on Cain. Anyone who saw the mark would know that Cain was protected by God. God still loved Cain and protected and cared for him.

—based on Genesis 4

Temptation

Cain should not have been angry at his brother. Because of original sin and its effects, it was hard for Cain to love his brother, to know what was right, and to choose what was right.

God wants us to be happy here on earth and some day with Him in heaven. God wants us to be free to choose to love Him and to be happy with Him. So, God created us in His image, with minds to think and wills to make choices. It is up to us to choose to love God and to accept the love and happiness He offers us.

When Adam and Eve committed the original sin, they were no longer able to love God as they should. It was difficult for them to know what was right and to make loving choices. Original sin and its effects were passed on to all the people who came after Adam and Eve, except Jesus and Mary. We are all conceived and born with original sin and its effects. It is still hard for us to know what is right and to make right choices. Sometimes we are tempted to make wrong choices.

> *Many "voices" inside and outside us tempt us not to believe in God, not to listen to His fatherly invitations, to prefer our whims to His friendship.*
> —Pope John Paul II

No matter whether temptations come from ourselves (for example, selfishness, emotions, weaknesses), from the world (people, places, and things), or from the devil, we can still choose to make right choices with the help of grace. But making right choices is difficult sometimes, and we struggle between what is right and what is wrong.

Read the following story situation. Then follow the directions given at the end of the story.

The Difficult Choice

IT was a beautiful, sunny, spring day. Andy, Mark, and John had to stay inside during recess and finish their science projects. Their teacher, Mrs. Brown, had warned the class about what would happen if they didn't have their work done on time, but the three boys hadn't listened. They chose to wait until the last minute to do their science projects, and they ran out of time. While the boys worked, Mrs. Brown wrote that night's homework assignment on the board, as she always did.

Andy worked especially hard. He knew he had put off doing his work, and he knew he had better finish this project, or he would be in trouble! Andy had already been to the principal's office several times, because he had not behaved in class. He had drawn pictures and written notes on the blackboard several times. If he got in trouble again, his parents would ground him for sure.

Mark and John usually got their work done on time, but with the beautiful spring weather, they had been busy playing baseball. Mark and John were best friends, and they played baseball together all the time. That's what they had planned to do at recess. John knew it was his own fault he had to stay in for recess, but Mark was really angry. Of all days for Mrs. Brown to keep them in!

Andy received permission to go to the bathroom. After he left, Mrs. Brown told Mark and John that she was going to go to the library to get a filmstrip and that she would be right back. She asked Mr. Carson, the other fourth-grade teacher, to look in on the boys.

When Mrs. Brown left, Mark quickly went up to the board, erased the homework assignment, and wrote "NO HOMEWORK!!" in its place. He was back at his desk working when Mr. Carson checked on the boys. As Mr. Carson was leaving, Andy returned and went back to his desk. He looked at the board to see how much homework Mrs. Brown had given them. When he saw "NO HOMEWORK!!" on the board, Andy knew Mrs. Brown would suspect him, because of the times he had written on the board before. Andy went up to the board to erase "NO HOMEWORK!!" Just as he got up to the board, Mrs. Brown walked in. She noticed the words written on the board in place of the homework assignment. Andy told Mrs. Brown that he hadn't written on the board, and that he didn't know who had. Mrs. Brown told Andy she was sorry, but his parents would have to be called, and his pranks would have to stop. Andy figured it was no use arguing, because he had written on the board other times. So he just sat at his desk.

Meanwhile, the rest of the class came in from recess as Mrs. Brown was rewriting the homework assignment. Mark worked at his desk with a little smirk on his face, because he had gotten by with his prank, and Andy had been blamed for it!

John, however, sat thinking. John knew that Mark had erased the homework assignment and had written "NO HOMEWORK!!" instead. John had watched Mark do it! John also knew that Andy was really in a lot of trouble this time. Andy was going to be punished for something Mark had done. John didn't know what to do. He didn't want Andy to get in trouble for something he didn't do. He also didn't want to tell on Mark, who was his best friend. Besides, if he told on Mark, Mark probably wouldn't be his friend anymore. Or maybe John should encourage Mark to tell Mrs. Brown the truth about what he did.

What was the right thing to do? If John helped Andy, he would betray his best friend, Mark. John had to make a choice. What will John do?

Put yourself in John's place and think about the choice he has to make. What would you do if you were John? Finish the story, telling the choice John makes and why he makes the choice he does.

_____

_____

_____

_____

_____

_____

_____

_____

_____

_____

_____

Sin and Forgiveness

Sometimes we fail to love as we should. Sometimes we are selfish, we give in to our weaknesses, we choose to sin. Sin is knowing something is wrong and choosing to do it anyway.

We know that by sin the Lord is offended, friendship with Him is broken, His grace is lost, one strays from the right path, heading for ruin.

Committing sin, we are far from God, against God, without God.
—Pope John Paul II

When we do sin, God still loves us. When we sin, we should tell God we are sorry and ask Him to forgive us. We should celebrate the sacrament of Reconciliation.

Psalm 25 is a prayer asking God for guidance and forgiveness. The following prayer is based on Psalm 25.

Prayer for Guidance and Help

To you I lift up my soul,
O LORD, my God.
In you I trust.

Help me to know and follow
your ways, O LORD.
Guide me in your truth and teach me,
for you are God my Savior.

You are compassionate and kind.
In your goodness, do not remember
my sins and my weaknesses.

You are honest and good, O LORD,
you show sinners the way.
You guide those who seek you,
and you teach them your way.

You offer your friendship
to those who show you great love and respect.
You free from sin
those who look toward you, O LORD,
and you instruct and guide them.

Look toward me
and have pity on me, O LORD.
My heart is deeply troubled,
and I am in great distress.

Remove my troubles and suffering
and take away all my sins.
Protect me, LORD,
I trust in your love and care.

6

God's Merciful Love

Does God love us even when we sin?
Yes, even when we sin, God still loves and cares for us. However, sin makes us less able to love God.

What is merciful love?
Merciful love is drawing good out of evil.

How does God show His merciful love?
God shows His merciful love when He forgives our sins. We, in turn, are grateful to God, and He draws us closer to Himself. The good that God draws from the evil of our sins is the fact that we turn back to God and have a closer relationship with Him.

> The LORD is gracious and merciful,
>   slow to anger and of great kindness.
> The LORD is good to all
>   and compassionate toward all his works.
>
> PSALM 145:8–9

Vocabulary

God's mercy: showing kindness and compassion; drawing good out of evil.
immoral: wrong, evil; indecent.
hospitality: welcome, cordiality.

God's Merciful Love

God is merciful and loving. Even when we sin, God continues to love us. However, we are less able to love God. We experience certain consequences of our sins. When we are sorry for our sins, God forgives us. We, in turn, are grateful to God, and He draws us closer to Himself. This is God's merciful love. The good that God draws from the evil of our sins is the fact that we turn back to God and have a closer relationship with Him.

God showed His merciful love to Adam and Eve by promising them a Savior and by providing them with clothing.

Cain experienced the consequences of killing Abel when he had to leave his home and wander from place to place. God showed Cain merciful love by protecting him and keeping him from harm.

God showed merciful love to Noah and his family by keeping them safe in the ark and caring for them.

When the people of Babylon forgot God as they worked on the tower of Babel, they began to speak different languages, and they moved away from Babel. God showed His merciful love by forming a new nation from among those people who were scattered.

God showed merciful love to Lot and his family by protecting Lot from the crowd that was trying to harm him. By the mercy of God, the angels removed Lot and his family bodily, by taking their hands and leading them out of the city, after first warning them that the city would be destroyed.

While God allows us to experience some of the consequences of our sins, He forgives our sins when we are sorry. We experience God's love and mercy. By experiencing God's love and mercy, we are grateful to God and draw closer to Him. By experiencing some consequences of our sins, we learn to be responsible for our actions. We can learn from our wrong choices and try to make right choices in the future.

We should thank God for the love and mercy He gives us in spite of the times we sin and do not love Him as we should.

King David, who lived before the time of Christ, praised and thanked God for the generosity God showed him and his country. The following prayer is based on Psalm 103, a prayer written by King David, praising God's goodness, mercy, and love.

Praise of God's Goodness

Bless the LORD, O my soul;
All my being, bless his holy name.
O my soul, bless the LORD;
   do not forget all he does for you.
He forgives all your sins,
   and heals all your ills.
He saves your life,
   and he treats you with kindness and compassion.

The LORD is just and right in all his actions.
He is merciful and gracious.
He is slow to anger and is filled with kindness.
He does not always scold us, nor does he stay angry.
He does not deal with us according to our sins.

The LORD's kindness to us is greater
   than the distance between heaven and earth.
The LORD has compassion on us
   as a father has compassion on his children.

The LORD's throne is in heaven,
   and his kingdom rules over all.
Bless the LORD, all you his angels,
You do what he asks and you love and obey him.
Bless the LORD, all his works,
everywhere in his kingdom.
Bless the LORD, O my soul.

God has always cared for each person, loving each one in a merciful way. God always forgives those who ask for forgiveness. As images of God, we should try to act as God does. We should try to love others and forgive those who ask for our forgiveness.

The following story is about a man who loved and forgave his brothers, even though he seemed to have a good reason not to.

Joseph and His Brothers

JACOB lived a long time ago. He and his family were shepherds. Jacob had twelve sons. He had a special love for his second-youngest son, whose name was Joseph. Jacob gave Joseph a beautiful coat. Then Joseph began to have dreams in which something or someone would bow down to him. He told his family about his dreams. Joseph's older brothers were very envious of him. They began to make plans to hurt him.

One day, Jacob sent Joseph out to the fields to check on his brothers. As Joseph was walking, his brothers saw him coming and made a plan to kill him. They said to one another, "Come on, let us kill him and throw him into one of the cisterns here; we could say that a wild beast devoured him."

One of Joseph's brothers, Reuben, tried to save him. He said, "We must not take his life. Don't kill him outright, just throw him into the well." The other brothers agreed to this plan. Reuben hoped to come back secretly later to rescue Joseph.

When Joseph arrived, the brothers grabbed him, tore off his coat, and threw him into the well, which was dry. Then they sat down to eat. As they were eating, a caravan of traders on their way to Egypt, came along. Judah, another of Joseph's brothers, said, "What is to be gained by killing our own brother? Let us sell him instead." The other brothers agreed, so they sold Joseph to the traders for twenty pieces of silver.

Then the brothers killed a goat. They took Joseph's coat, soaked it in goat's blood, and took it to their father. Jacob recognized the coat right away. "Joseph has been torn to pieces", cried Jacob. He was sure a wild beast had devoured Joseph.

Meanwhile, Joseph was taken into Egypt and sold to a friend of the Pharaoh. Joseph's master put Joseph in charge of his household. The master's wife tricked Joseph and, because of her trick, Joseph was put into jail. While in jail, Joseph was put in charge of the other prisoners.

Two of the prisoners were men who had worked for the Pharaoh. One morning, Joseph saw that these men were upset. He asked, "Why do you look so sad today?" They replied that they had had bad dreams. The two men told Joseph about their dreams. Joseph explained to them what the dreams meant. What Joseph told them would happen, did happen. One of the men went free and went back to work for the Pharaoh.

Two years went by, and Joseph was still in prison. One night the Pharaoh had a dream. He saw seven fat cows grazing on green grass. Behind them, he saw seven ugly, skinny cows, who came and ate the seven fat cows. The dream woke the Pharaoh, but he quickly fell back to sleep and had another dream. This time he saw seven ears of fat, healthy grain. Then he saw seven thin ears sprout up and swallow the healthy ears.

When the Pharaoh woke up, he was upset. He called all his advisors and told them about his dreams. He wanted one of them to interpret or explain the dreams. No one was able to interpret the dreams. Then the worker who had been in prison with Joseph told the Pharaoh about him. "When we told him our dreams, he interpreted them for us and explained for each of us the meaning of his dream", said the worker.

Pharaoh quickly summoned Joseph from the prison. Pharaoh said, "I had certain dreams that no one can interpret. But I hear it said of you that the moment you are told a dream you can interpret it."

"It is not I," Joseph replied, "but God who will give Pharaoh the right answer." Then Joseph listened to Pharaoh tell about his dreams. Joseph explained, "Both of Pharaoh's dreams have the same meaning. God has thus foretold to Pharaoh what he is about to do. The seven healthy cows are seven years, and the seven healthy ears are seven years—the same in each dream. So also the seven thin, ugly cows that came up after them are seven years, as are the seven thin, wind-blasted ears; they are seven years of famine. It is just as I told Pharaoh: God has revealed to Pharaoh what he is about to do. Seven years of great abundance are now coming throughout the land of Egypt; but these will be followed by seven years of famine, when all the abundance in the land of Egypt will be forgotten."

Joseph advised Pharaoh to put a wise man in charge of the land of Egypt. Joseph advised him to store grain in all the towns during the good years. The stored grain would serve as a reserve during the seven years of famine. Pharaoh said, "Since God has made all this known to you, no one can be as wise and discerning as you are. You shall be in charge of my palace and all my people shall dart at your command."

During the next seven years, Joseph traveled throughout Egypt. He collected the abundant food and stored it in all the nearby towns. Joseph thought that he was a lucky man. He married and had two sons. Joseph named his oldest son Manasseh, meaning "God has made me forget entirely the suffering I endured at the hands of my family"; and he named his second son Ephraim, meaning "God has made me fruitful in the land of my affliction."

After seven years of abundance, the great famine set in. The famine affected many countries. Only Egypt had enough food for its people. Joseph rationed food to the Egyptian people. Soon people from all over the world came to Egypt to obtain rations of grain. Because Joseph was the governor, they had to ask him for their rations.

Back home, Jacob said to his sons, "I hear that rations of grain are available in Egypt. Go down there and buy some for us, that we may stay alive rather than die of hunger." So all of Joseph's brothers, except for the youngest, Benjamin, left for Egypt. Jacob would not let Benjamin go, because he was afraid something would happen to him.

When the brothers arrived in Egypt, they went to Joseph, who recognized them immediately. However, the brothers did not recognize Joseph. Joseph remembered the dreams he had had about them. Joseph said, "You are spies."

His brothers replied, "No governor! We have come to ask for some food. We are twelve brothers, sons of Jacob in Canaan. The youngest is with our father, and the other one is gone."

Joseph insisted that the brothers were indeed spies. He said, "This is how you shall be tested: unless your youngest brother comes here, I swear by the life of Pharaoh that you shall not leave here. So send one of your number to get your brother, while the rest of you stay here under arrest." With that, he locked them up for three days.

On the third day Joseph went to them and said, "Only one of your brothers need be confined in this prison, while the rest of you may go and take home provisions for your starving families. But you must come back to me with your youngest brother." Joseph's brothers agreed to this. They thought they were being punished because of what they had done to Joseph.

Joseph understood what they were thinking. He turned away and began to cry. When Joseph was able to speak again, he ordered his brother Simeon to be taken away. Then Joseph had his brothers' containers filled with grain. He also returned their money, hiding it among their belongings.

When the brothers arrived home, they found their money. They told Jacob everything that had happened. Jacob was afraid that something would happen to Benjamin, so Jacob would not let him go.

The famine became worse. Soon the family had used up all the rations the brothers had brought back from Egypt. Jacob told them to go back to Egypt for more food. They refused to go unless Benjamin went with them. Jacob knew they needed the food, so he finally agreed. He said, "If it must be so then do this: Put some of the land's best products in your baggage and take them down to the man as gifts." He also told them to take some extra money along to pay back the money that had been put into their bags by mistake. Then they left for Egypt.

When Joseph saw his brothers with Benjamin, he turned to one of his servants and told him to prepare a special dinner. The brothers were brought into the house. They presented Joseph with the gifts they had brought. Then Joseph instructed them where to sit. The brothers were amazed, because they were seated according to their age, from oldest to youngest.

After dinner, Joseph told his servant to fill the brothers' bags with as much food as possible and to put each man's money back into his bag. Joseph also told the servant to put Joseph's silver goblet into Benjamin's bag.

The next morning the brothers left for home. Joseph told his head servant to go after them. Joseph told him, "Go at once after the men. When you overtake them, say to them, 'Why did you repay good with evil? Why did you steal the silver goblet from me? What you have done is wrong.'"

When the servant caught up with the brothers, he repeated Joseph's words. They exclaimed, "Why would we steal silver and gold from your master's house? We even brought back to you from the land of Canaan the money we found in our bags."

The servant told them that he had to search their bags. He explained that the one who had the silver goblet would have to come back and become a slave. He searched everyone's bag and finally found the goblet in the last bag, Benjamin's bag.

The whole group then went back to the city. When they reached Joseph's house, the brothers pleaded with Joseph. Joseph said, "Only the one in whose possession the goblet was found shall become my slave. The rest of you may go back safe and sound to your father."

Judah begged Joseph to let Benjamin go. He explained that one of their brothers was dead and that Benjamin was very special to their father. Judah said, "How could I go back to my father if the boy were not with me? I could not bear to see the anguish that would overcome my father."

Joseph could no longer keep his secret. "I am Joseph", he said to his brothers. "Is my father in good health?"

The brothers were so surprised they could not move or speak. Joseph said, "I am your brother Joseph, whom you once sold into Egypt. But now do not be distressed, and do not reproach yourselves for having sold me here. It was really for the sake of saving lives that God sent me ahead of you.

"Hurry back, then to my father and tell him: 'Thus says your son Joseph: God has made me lord of all Egypt; come to me without delay. . . . Since five years of famine still lie ahead, I will provide for you there, so that you and your family and all that are yours may not suffer want.'"

Then Joseph hugged Benjamin tightly, and they both began to cry. Joseph then kissed each of his brothers. The brothers brought Jacob and the rest of their family to Egypt. They were given some land to live on.

—based on Genesis 37–45

Joseph had great reason to be angry with his brothers. First, they plotted to kill him. Then they sold him to some men traveling to Egypt. Imagine what Joseph must have felt when his own brothers sold him. He probably thought he would never see his family again. However, Joseph knew that God would be always with him. Joseph forgave his brothers for everything. He even helped them during the famine. Joseph helped them move to Egypt.

Joseph showed merciful love toward his brothers. He continued to love them and to forgive them in spite of what they had done to him. We should do the same thing. We should show merciful love toward others.

What are ways we can show merciful love?

Example: *My friend lied and told the teacher that I had stolen his football, when he himself lost it. I can forgive my friend and not stay angry at him.*

Give three examples of your own:

1 _____

_____

_____

2 _____

_____

_____

3 _____

_____

_____

Match column A with column B.

A	B

____ Tower of Babel

____ Noah and the Great Flood

____ Adam and Eve (original sin)

____ Lot and His Family

____ Cain's Wrong Choice

____ Joseph and His Brothers

1 God provided them with clothes and other things. They must have been grateful to Him. Their gratitude drew them closer to God.

2 These people were saved when the cities were destroyed. They must have been grateful to God. Their gratitude drew them closer to Him.

3 God protected him as he wandered from place to place. He must have been grateful to God. His gratitude drew him closer to God.

4 He forgave his brothers for selling him into slavery.

5 The people forgot about God. They were full of pride. The people were scattered and began to speak different languages. God showed His merciful love by forming a new nation from among the scattered peoples.

6 God protected him and his family in an ark. God established a covenant with him and his descendants. This new bond of love is the good that God draws from the evil of sin.

Unit 3

Jesus,
Our Example

7

Jesus' Loving Example

CONCEPTS OF FAITH

What does Jesus as Priest show us?
How we should act and how we should offer sacrifice to God to show love for God and others. He also shows us that we should forgive others as He forgives us.

Why did God the Son become man?
God the Son became man to teach us who we are and to show us how we should act as images of God. He became man to return the Father's love and to help us to return God's love.

Jesus came to this earth to show us and to guarantee to us God's love. He came to love us and to be loved. Let yourselves be loved by Christ!

POPE JOHN PAUL II

Vocabulary

priest: one who offers sacrifices to God to show love for God and others.

to will: to choose.

self-discipline: control of one's emotions, desires, or actions by one's own will.

account: a detailed list of what one owes.

Jesus as Priest

Because Adam and Eve sinned, they wounded their abilities to think and to choose. They did not always act as images of God. They lost grace, and they were not able to return God's love. God promised Adam and Eve that He would send a Savior. Jesus, God the Son, is our Savior. Only Jesus could make up for original sin and all other sins. Only Jesus could repair our relationship with God, because only Jesus is both God and man.

Jesus came to teach us who we are and show us how we should act as images of God. He came to return the Father's love and to help us to return God's love.

A priest is one who offers sacrifices to God to show love for God and others. Jesus as Priest shows us, by His example, how we should act. He shows us how we should offer ourselves in sacrifice to show love for God and others. Jesus also shows us that we should forgive others as He forgives us.

Ordained priests are men who have answered God's call and have chosen to offer their lives to God and to act as helpers to the bishop. Ordained priests serve our Church communities. They celebrate Eucharist and some of the other sacraments and teach us about God.

The priestly role we might not be familiar with is the priestly role that Jesus calls us to through our Baptism.

Through Baptism, we share in the priestly office of Christ. As priests we should offer ourselves in sacrifice to show love for God and others. We should also forgive others as God forgives us. We receive the power to act as priests in Baptism. The power to act as priests is called love. Love comes to us along with the grace of Baptism.

Jesus as Priest shows us, by His example, how we should act as baptized priests. He shows us how we should offer ourselves in sacrifice to show love for God and others. Jesus also shows us that we should forgive others as He forgives us.

While Jesus was on earth, He loved and cared for the people. He healed the sick, the lame, and the blind. He was merciful and forgave people's sins. (When Jesus healed people physically, He usually forgave their sins.)

Look through the Gospel of Matthew. Find a story that tells of a time when Jesus showed love, mercy, and forgiveness. Write the story in your own words in the space below. Indicate the chapter and verses of the story.

Jesus' Sacrifice of Love

LATE in the evening, after the Last Supper, Jesus was arrested by soldiers and others. The soldiers made fun of Jesus. They whipped Him many times, covering His back with bleeding wounds. The soldiers made a crown out of thorns and put it on Jesus' head. Then Pontius Pilate gave the order to have Jesus crucified.

Jesus was given a Cross. He had to carry this Cross to a place called Golgotha, which is just outside the city of Jerusalem. This walk must have been very hard for Jesus. The soldiers made a man, Simon the Cyrenian, help carry the Cross to Golgotha.

When they arrived at Golgotha, the soldiers nailed Jesus to the Cross. Pilate had a sign made that said, "Jesus the Nazorean, the King of the Jews". This sign was put on the Cross above Jesus' head.

Two thieves were also crucified with Jesus—one on His right, and the other on His left.

There was a crowd of people gathered at the place of crucifixion. Some of the people were friends of Jesus, who believed in Him. Other people were not friends of Jesus. They made fun of Him, saying, "He saved others, let him save himself if he is the chosen one, the Messiah of God." Jesus prayed, "Father, forgive them, they know not what they do."

One of the thieves cried out to Jesus, saying, "Are you not the Messiah? Save yourself and us." This thief was not sorry for the crime he had committed.

The other thief knew that what he had done was wrong. This good thief was sorry for what he had done. The good thief scolded the other thief. He reminded him that they were receiving the just punishment for their crimes, but that Jesus had done nothing wrong.

Then the good thief looked at Jesus and said, "Jesus, remember me when you come into your kingdom." Jesus then promised the good thief that he would be with Him in heaven.

Mary, Jesus' Mother, and some friends of Jesus stood near the Cross. John, one of the Apostles, was also there. Jesus saw them standing there.

Jesus said to His Mother, "Woman, behold, your son." Then Jesus spoke to John, "Behold, your mother." From then on, John cared for Mary.

Around twelve o'clock in the afternoon, darkness came over the land. At about three o'clock, Jesus cried out in a loud voice, "My God, my God, why have you forsaken me?"

One of the onlookers soaked a sponge in some wine and, putting it on a stick, gave Jesus a drink. After tasting the wine, Jesus said, "Father, into your hands I commend my spirit." After Jesus said these words, He died.

—based on Matthew 27:51–66; Luke 23:26–47; John 19:1–30

The Love of Jesus

We see in Jesus' suffering and death a perfect act of love. As Priest, Jesus loves us in a merciful way. Jesus freely chose to suffer and to lay down His life according to His Father's will. Jesus willed every lash of the whip, every thorn in the crown, and every fall as He carried the Cross. Jesus offered Himself to show love for the Father and for us.

In His suffering and death, Jesus shows us that God is loving, merciful, and forgiving. Jesus loves, and He shows us how to love. When we see the love of Jesus, we know how we should love God and others.

Sometimes we make wrong choices and do not love God and others as we should. When we make wrong choices, we should seek God's merciful love and forgiveness in the sacrament of Reconciliation.

In the letter to the Hebrews it is written of Jesus:

For we do not have a high priest who is unable to sympathize with our weaknesses, but one who has similarly been tested in every way, yet without sin. So let us confidently approach the throne of grace to receive mercy and to find grace for timely help.
—Hebrews 4:15–16

Dying on the Cross, Jesus loved us with a merciful love. Jesus saved us from original sin and from all other sins. He repaired our relationship with God and drew us closer to Him.

Jesus as Priest loves, and He shows us how to love God and others, by offering Himself in sacrifice.

Through our Baptism we are called to imitate Jesus in His priestly role. We should imitate the merciful love of Jesus by loving God and by loving and forgiving others as Jesus loves and forgives us.

Almost two thousand years ago, Saint Paul wrote a letter to a group of people called the Colossians, reminding them how they should act as images of God.

Put on then, as God's chosen ones, holy and beloved, heartfelt compassion, kindness, humility, gentleness, and patience, bearing with one another and forgiving one another, if one has a grievance against another; as the Lord has forgiven you, so must you also do. And over all these put on love, that is, the bond of perfection. And let the peace of Christ control your hearts, the peace into which you were also called in one body. And be thankful. Let the word of Christ dwell in you richly, as in all wisdom you teach and admonish one another, singing psalms, hymns, and spiritual songs with gratitude in your hearts to God. And whatever you do, in word and in deed, do everything in the name of the Lord Jesus, giving thanks to God the Father through him.
—Colossians 3:12–17

What Saint Paul said in his letter is just as important for us today as it was for the people back then.

8

Jesus Teaches Us
the Truth

What is a prophet?
A prophet is someone who, through words and actions, gives witness to the truth about God.

What does Jesus as Prophet teach us?
He teaches us who we are—images of God. He teaches us the truth about God.

You children, always be strongly united with Christ the Truth. Be witnesses to the Truth, which is He Himself and His message, entrusted to man who is frail and strong at the same time. Beloved boys and girls! Christ is waiting for you to free you from evil, sin, and error; that is, from the real roots from which come the miseries that lower and shame man. Always be prophets and witnesses to the Truth!

POPE JOHN PAUL II

Vocabulary

prophet: someone who, through words and actions, gives witness to the truth about God.
prophecy: words spoken through divine inspiration.

The Greatest Prophet

A prophet is someone who reveals the truth about God. Jesus is the greatest prophet. Out of His love for us, God the Father sent God the Son to teach us the truth about God. Throughout His life, Jesus the Prophet told us the truth about God. He told people who they were—images of God.

Read the following passage from Scripture, in which Jesus tells us that He is the Savior Whom God the Father had promised to send.

Jesus the Prophet

ONE day, Jesus arrived in Nazareth, the town where He had grown up. As was His custom, He went to the synagogue on the Sabbath. He stood up to read. Jesus was handed a scroll of the prophet Isaiah. He unrolled the scroll and read, "The Spirit of the Lord is upon me, because he has anointed me to bring glad tidings to the poor. He has sent me to proclaim liberty to captives and recovery of sight to the blind, to let the oppressed go free, and to proclaim a year acceptable to the Lord."

Jesus then rolled up the scroll and handed it back to the attendant. Everyone looked at Jesus. He said, "Today this Scripture passage is fulfilled in your hearing." Everyone was amazed at Jesus' words. They knew Him only as a carpenter's son. They said, "Isn't this the son of Joseph?"

Jesus answered, "Amen, I say to you, no prophet is accepted in his own native place."

—based on Luke 4:16–24

In this story, Jesus was informing the people that He was the one to fulfill this prophecy of Isaiah.

Jesus came to reveal the truth about God to us. He tells us that God always speaks the truth. Jesus reveals that God is loving and gentle. Jesus teaches us Who God is and teaches us who we are.

Before Jesus began His work, the devil tempted Him to make wrong choices. Jesus was able to respond to the devil's lies with the truth, because He is the Truth.

The Temptation of Jesus

Jesus went into the desert, where He spent forty days and forty nights to prepare Himself before beginning His work. During this time, Jesus fasted. Jesus also prayed to God the Father and thought about the work He was to begin.

After fasting, Jesus was very hungry. The devil knew how hungry Jesus was. The devil said to Jesus, "If you are the Son of God, command that these stones become loaves of bread." Jesus told the devil the truth, that in order to live people needed more than food. Living means more than eating. It means acting as an image of God and doing the Father's will. Christ always acted as an image of God, so He did not do what the devil asked.

Jesus let the devil take Him to Jerusalem and set Him on the roof of the temple. The devil told Jesus that He could jump off the rooftop and not get hurt, because God the Father had promised He would send angels to care for Jesus. The devil wanted Jesus to test His Father's truthfulness. Jesus told the devil that we should not test God the Father. God always loves and cares for us and tells us the truth.

Finally, Jesus let the devil take Him to the top of a very high mountain. The devil showed Jesus all the lands and riches of the world. The devil told Jesus that all these things could be His if Jesus would worship him, the devil. But Jesus told the devil to leave. Jesus told the devil the truth, that is, we should worship only God. The devil is not God. Only God deserves our worship.

Then the devil left Jesus. Angels came to Jesus and cared for Him.
—based on Matthew 4:1–11

Temptations

The devil tempted Jesus the way he tempted Adam and Eve. Adam and Eve made the wrong choice. They listened to the devil and believed his lies. They didn't trust God the Father. Jesus made the right choice and did not listen to the devil's lies. He trusted God the Father and knew that the Father always tells the truth.

Sometimes we are tempted to make wrong choices, too. We should not listen to these temptations. They are lies. We should always trust God the Father. We know from what Jesus taught us that God the Father always loves and cares for us and tells us the truth.

Jesus came to tell us the truth about God. The devil tempted Jesus with lies about God, just as he had tempted Adam and Eve with lies about God. The devil tempted Adam and Eve by telling them that they should not trust God. God told Adam and Eve that, if they ate fruit of the tree of good and evil, they could not live with Him in heaven. But the devil told Adam and Eve that, if they ate fruit of the tree of good and evil, they would become like gods. As gods, they would be able to say what was good or evil. They would no longer have to listen to God to learn what was good or evil. Adam and Eve chose not to listen to God and to accept the devil's lie. They sinned. When Jesus was tempted in the desert, He refused to accept the devil's lies. Instead, Jesus, as a prophet, reveals the truth about God. The truth is that God can be trusted, and that we should listen to Him and act as images of Him.

List three ways Jesus was tempted.

- _____
- _____
- _____

What truths did Jesus teach us when He refused to accept the devil's lies?

_____

_____

_____

_____

_____

G R A C E

F A I T H

The Grace of Baptism

Through Baptism, we share in the prophetic office of Christ. As prophets, we should give witness to the truth about God. But we need to know the truth before we can give witness to it. The truth is found in the Sacred Scriptures and the teachings of the Church. We receive the power to believe the truth in Baptism. This power to believe is called faith, and faith comes to us along with grace in Baptism.

Once we know the truth, then we should act as prophets by giving witness to the truth. Through our words and actions, we should share the truth that we believe. Like Jesus, we should give witness to the truth, even when it is difficult to do so. Through our words and actions, we should help others to understand that God is trustworthy, that He is a loving, caring Father, and that people should act as images of God.

Think of stories in which Jesus taught us that God is a loving, caring, and trusting Father. List seven stories.

1 _____

2 _____

3 _____

4 _____

5 _____

6 _____

7 _____

Read the following story. In this story, does someone act as a prophet? Does this person teach the truth to other people?

A Witness to the Truth

JOEY, Tom, and Jeff went to play basketball at the gym on Saturday. When they arrived at the gym, the rest of the team was standing outside. "Why aren't you practicing on the court?" asked Tom.

"Because there are some eighth-graders playing, and they won't let us in the gym," explained Cory.

"But we signed up for this time. They can't take it from us. It wouldn't be fair," yelled Joey.

"You try to explain that to them. They're bigger than us, and there are more of them. They're acting like bullies!" said Sean.

Joey, Tom, and Jeff walked into the gym. Jeff approached the older boys. "Excuse me, but I think there's been a mistake. This is our hour to use the gym. Why don't you check the schedule. You'll see that we have signed up for this time." The older boys laughed. One of them said, "We don't pay any attention to the schedule. We are more important than other kids, and we use the gym whenever we want to. Now scram, you're keeping us from our fun!"

Joey said, "No, it's you that's keeping us from our fun, so you leave." At that, the older boys picked up the three younger boys (Joey, Jeff, and Tom) and carried them outside. Then they blocked the door so the boys could not get back into the gym. The boys did not know what to do. They knew that the older boys were wrong, but what could they do about it? They decided to go to the video arcade and have some fun there. As they walked, they decided to take a shortcut across Mr. Peters' garden. In the garden were some pumpkin vines with flowers, some carrots starting to sprout, and large corn stalks with tiny ears of corn starting to grow. Joey started to pull up some of the carrots. Tom plucked some flowers off the pumpkin vines. Soon everyone was pulling at the plants, except Jeff.

Jeff tried to get them to stop. "Hey, guys. Mr. Peters has worked hard in this garden. He always raises the largest pumpkins in the city. Leave things alone."

No one would listen to Jeff. "Jeff, knock it off and have some fun. Who cares about Mr. Peters? He's not our friend!" said Sean. "Besides, what is he going to do? There are more of us, and we're a lot stronger than one old man!"

Jeff looked at his friends for a moment. "Then I'm going home. You guys sound just like the eighth-graders at the gym", exploded Jeff. "There were more of them, and they were bigger than us, so they could be mean and rude, and we couldn't stop them! So they thought it was okay to bully us. Now you guys are doing the same thing! Well, it is wrong. It's wrong for the older boys to pick on us, and it's wrong for us to pick on Mr. Peters." Jeff left his friends and went home.

The other boys stopped what they were doing. It was hard for them to admit it, but they knew Jeff was right. "What should we do?" asked Joey. "Let's go buy some seeds and replant Mr. Peters' garden", suggested Tom. "We'd better apologize to Mr. Peters, too", said Cory.

Later, the boys went to Jeff's house. Joey said, "Jeff, we're sorry we called you names. You were the one who was right. We just didn't care about Mr. Peters, and we should have. It took guts for you to stand up to all your friends."

Jeff was glad to see his friends, and they went outside and played football.

Jeff acted as a prophet and witnessed to the truths that Jesus taught. Jesus taught us not to damage someone else's property and to love others. Put yourself in Jeff's place. It was probably hard for him to witness to the truth, to stand up to his friends, and to walk away from them. But he did it, because he knew it was the right choice. Jeff acted as an image of God should.

9

Jesus, the King, Rules with Love

CONCEPTS OF FAITH

What does Jesus as King show us?
He shows us God's love in and through His human body. He shows us self-discipline and how we should use the things of creation for the benefit of all people.

What sacrament first calls us to act as priests, prophets, and kings?
Baptism.

The message of love that Christ brought is always important, always up-to-date. It is not difficult to see how today's world is thirsting for more truth, for more love, for more joy. And all of this is found in Christ and in His way of life. In whatever you do, remember that Christ is calling you, in one way or another, to the service of love: the love of God and of your neighbor.

POPE JOHN PAUL II

Vocabulary

king: one who governs or rules.

self-discipline: control of one's emotions, desires, or actions by one's own will.

deacons: men who have received Holy Orders for the diaconate, who practice self-discipline, who serve the Church, and who use the things of the world for the benefit of others.

ordained: to become a deacon, priest, or bishop by receiving the sacrament of Holy Orders.

What Is a King?

A king is one who governs or rules. A good king is just, fair, kind, self-controlled, unselfish, and concerned about the people he rules.

A king who is selfish would not be kind to, or concerned about, the people he rules. He would not care if the people had food and shelter or if they were poor or sick.

A king who does not control his emotions would not be just or fair. His feelings would affect his actions. For example, if he made an important decision or ruling when he was angry, the decision or ruling might not be a good one and might hurt the country and the people he rules.

Think of a king or leader who did not rule a country well. Did some of the decisions made by the king or leader hurt the country and the people in the country? In the space below, write about a king or leader who did not rule well.

_____

_____

_____

_____

_____

_____

A good king governs himself first, by controlling his emotions, desires, and actions. A good king respects, cares for, and is concerned about the people he rules. He uses the things of the earth to provide for the needs of his people. Think of a king or leader who ruled a country well. Did the decisions made by the king or leader help and show concern for the country and the people in the country? In the space below, write about a king or leader who ruled well.

_____

_____

_____

_____

_____

_____

Jesus as King

Jesus as King shows us God's truth and love in and through His human body. As King, Jesus governs Himself with self-discipline (self-control). He controls His emotions, desires, and actions.

We see Jesus' control over His emotions when He was standing before the Roman governor, Pontius Pilate. Jesus must have experienced fear as He was questioned by Pilate. Yet, when Pilate asked Jesus if He was a king, Jesus' kingly self-control made it possible for Him to overcome fear and speak the truth.

We see Jesus' kingly self-control in His suffering and death on the Cross. Knowing how He would suffer and die, Jesus must have felt fearful and anxious in the Garden of Gethsemane. With His kingly self-control, Jesus was able to overcome His feelings of fear and anxiety. He was able to choose the pain and suffering of His Passion and death.

With His kingly self-control, Jesus was able to do things that must have been very difficult for Him.

Write about a time when you made a right choice and did what was right, even though it was hard for you to do the right thing.

I had a really bad headache and my dad asked me to take out my dog and so I took him out.

Jesus Rules over Creation

After Adam and Eve sinned, they found it difficult to rule over creation. They had to leave the Garden of Eden, and they had to work hard for their food and clothing. They needed to be shown how to rule over creation and to use the things of the earth for the good of others.

Jesus as King rules over all creation, and He uses the things of the earth for the good of all people.

We see Jesus' kingly rule over the things of the earth when He multiplied the fish and the loaves of bread to feed the thousands of people who came one day to listen to Him speak. He used the loaves and fish to benefit all the people by feeding them. We also see Jesus' rule over creation when He calmed a storm.

Jesus Calms the Storm

ONE day, after Jesus had been teaching the people, a crowd continued to surround Him. Jesus was very tired. So He asked His disciples to take Him to the other shore of the lake, where He could find some rest. He got into the boat with His disciples. Jesus sat down, rested His head, and fell into a very sound sleep.

As the small boat made its way across the lake, clouds suddenly appeared. They were big, threatening clouds. Without warning, the wind started blowing violently. Waves tossed the boat around as though it were a toy. The sky became very dark, only to be lit up with great streaks of lightning. Thunder echoed across the water. And the disciples in their small boat thought they were going to die.

Jesus continued to sleep, in spite of all that was happening around Him. The disciples frantically woke Him from His sleep, crying, "Teacher, do you not care that we are perishing?"

Jesus asked them, "Why are you terrified? Do you not yet have faith?" Then He stood up, and in a commanding voice He addressed the wind and sea, saying "Quiet! Be still!"

The wind stopped blowing, and the sea became calm. The disciples were dumbfounded. They said to one another, "Who then is this, whom even wind and sea obey?"

—based on Mark 4:35–41

Jesus calmed the storm to show that He is God and to show His authority over creation. However, He also calmed the storm to relieve the fears of His disciples. In other words, Jesus, through His kingly office, showed us that God governs all things for the sake of people.

Psalm 96 praises the Lord, the King of the Universe.

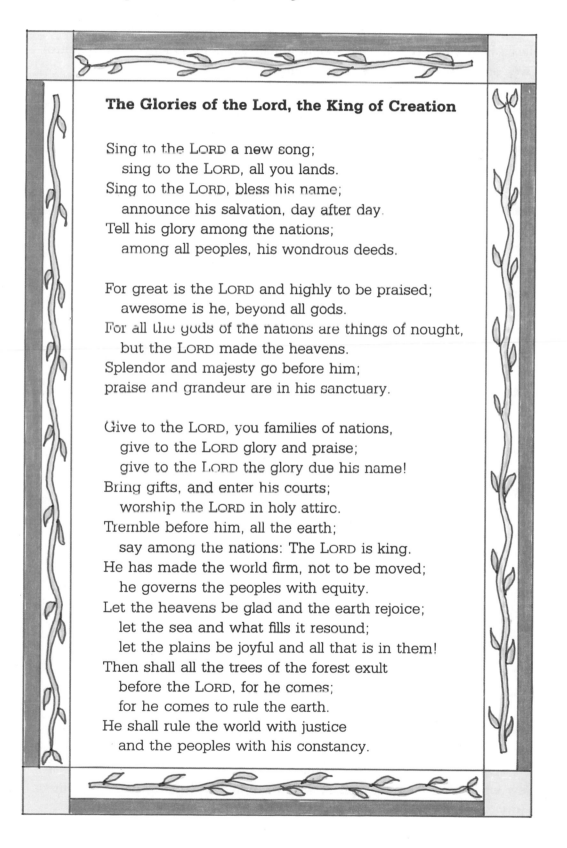

The Glories of the Lord, the King of Creation

Sing to the LORD a new song;
    sing to the LORD, all you lands.
Sing to the LORD, bless his name;
    announce his salvation, day after day.
Tell his glory among the nations;
    among all peoples, his wondrous deeds.

For great is the LORD and highly to be praised;
    awesome is he, beyond all gods.
For all the gods of the nations are things of nought,
    but the LORD made the heavens.
Splendor and majesty go before him;
praise and grandeur are in his sanctuary.

Give to the LORD, you families of nations,
    give to the LORD glory and praise;
    give to the LORD the glory due his name!
Bring gifts, and enter his courts;
    worship the LORD in holy attire.
Tremble before him, all the earth;
    say among the nations: The LORD is king.
He has made the world firm, not to be moved;
    he governs the peoples with equity.
Let the heavens be glad and the earth rejoice;
    let the sea and what fills it resound;
    let the plains be joyful and all that is in them!
Then shall all the trees of the forest exult
    before the LORD, for he comes;
    for he comes to rule the earth.
He shall rule the world with justice
    and the peoples with his constancy.

We Imitate Jesus

Jesus shows us God's love and truth in and through His human body—in and through His actions. As King, Jesus uses self-control and governs Himself, and He governs creation. Jesus uses the things of the earth for our benefit. When we imitate Jesus by doing these things, we show love and truth in and through our human bodies—in and through our actions.

When we are baptized, we are made kings and are called to imitate Jesus in His kingly role. We should imitate Jesus by practicing self-control over our emotions, desires, and feelings.

We are also called to rule over creation and to use material goods for the benefit of others. We receive the powers to act as kings in Baptism. The powers to practice self-control, to rule over creation, and to use material things for the good of other people are fortitude and temperance. Fortitude and temperance come to us along with the grace of Baptism.

A STORY OF FAITH

A man named Stephen was a disciple of Jesus. In the following story we see how Stephen imitated Jesus as a priest, prophet, and king.

Saint Stephen

AFTER Jesus ascended into heaven, the Apostles went out and taught the people about Him.

Many of the people believed in Jesus and became Christians. The number of Christians grew every day. Some of the people who became Christians were Jews who spoke Hebrew or Aramaic. Many others were Jews who spoke only Greek.

It was the custom of the early Christians to share everything in common. All the food, clothing, land, and cattle belonged to the whole Christian community. Everything was shared among all the people.

One day, some men from the group of Jews who spoke only Greek went to speak with the Apostles. They explained to the Apostles that the Hebrew-speaking Jews were not giving them a fair share of food and other items.

The Apostles could not take time away from their teaching to settle these kinds of problems. So, the Apostles ordained seven men as deacons to distribute food and see to the other material needs of the people.

The Apostles prayed and laid their hands on the seven men. They asked God to bless the men and give them the power to perform the tasks for which they had been chosen.

One of the seven men appointed was named Stephen. Stephen was a Jew who spoke Greek. Stephen, who was filled with faith, grace, and the Holy Spirit, worked great signs and wonders among the people.

One day, when Stephen was teaching about Jesus, some people who did not believe in Jesus argued with Stephen. Then they decided to accuse Stephen of speaking in the name of Jesus and speaking against God and the law of Moses. They brought Stephen before the Sanhedrin, Jewish leaders who did not believe in Jesus. Stephen spoke to the Sanhedrin, telling them about the history of the Jewish people, beginning with the time of Abraham. He spoke about Moses and how he was rejected by the people. He also spoke about the prophets who told about the coming of Christ and how they were put to death.

Then Stephen said to them, "You stiff-necked people, . . . you always oppose the holy Spirit; you are just like your ancestors." Then Stephen reminded the Jewish leaders that they had had Jesus, God the Son, put to death.

When the people heard this, they were very angry. Stephen, who was filled with the Holy Spirit, looked up to heaven and saw the glory of God and Jesus standing at the right hand of God. Stephen said, "Behold, I see the heavens opened and the Son of Man standing at the right hand of God."

At this the people became furious. They rushed at Stephen and threw him out of the city. Then they began to stone him. Stephen called out, "Lord Jesus, receive my spirit." Then, just before he died, Stephen cried out in a loud voice, "Lord, do not hold this sin against them."

—based on Acts 6 and 7

We see Stephen acting as priest, prophet, and king. We see Stephen as priest in his love and care for people, as he forgives the people as they stone him, and as he offers his life for love of God. We see Stephen as prophet as he teaches the people the truth about Jesus, and especially as he speaks before the Sanhedrin. We see Stephen as king as he uses things for the benefit of the Christian community and in the self-discipline he exercises as he speaks before the Sanhedrin and as he is stoned.

10

We Help Each Other

What is a corporal work of mercy?
An act of love we do that helps others with their physical needs.

What are the seven corporal works of mercy?
1. To feed the hungry.
2. To give drink to the thirsty.
3. To clothe the naked.
4. To visit those who are in prison.
5. To shelter the homeless.
6. To visit the sick.
7. To bury the dead.

What is a spiritual work of mercy?
An act of love we show to others to help them in their spiritual needs.

What are the seven spiritual works of mercy?
1. To admonish the sinner.
2. To instruct the ignorant.
3. To counsel the doubtful.
4. To comfort the sorrowful.
5. To bear wrongs patiently.
6. To forgive all injuries.
7. To pray for the living and the dead.

Love Jesus especially in those who are suffering in any way: physically, morally, spiritually. Let it be your duty and program to love your neighbor, discovering Christ's face in him.

POPE JOHN PAUL II

righteous: in union with God's will.

admonish: to caution someone against making a wrong choice.

Jesus Tells Us How to Treat Others

At the end of time, Jesus will come to judge the living and the dead. To some of us, Jesus will say, "Come, you who are blessed by my Father. Inherit the kingdom prepared for you from the foundation of the world. For I was hungry and you gave me food, I was thirsty and you gave me drink, a stranger and you welcomed me, naked and you clothed me, ill and you cared for me, in prison and you visited me." Then the righteous will answer him and say, "Lord, when did we see you hungry and feed you, or thirsty and give you drink? When did we see you a stranger and welcome you, or naked and clothe you? When did we see you ill or in prison, and visit you?" And the king [Jesus] will say to them in reply, "Amen, I say to you, whatever you did for one of these least brothers of mine, you did for me." (Based on Matthew 25:31–41.)

The corporal works of mercy are acts of love that help others with their physical needs. When we do these acts, we act the way Jesus did.

How can we feed the hungry?

We hear on the radio or television or we read in the paper about the people who are hungry in our city, our country, or the world. We know that these people need help, and we wonder what we can do for them.

We can help by praying for them. We can also help at the local food shelf, by sorting food and getting food ready to hand out. Sometimes our parish collects money for missions, and we can donate some of our own money. We know there are poor people in our own city. We can participate in a food drive for them.

How can we give drink to the thirsty?

We should always be kind to people who are in need. As images of God we should help people as Jesus helped them when He was on earth. One way we can help is by sharing our milk with a classmate who forgot to bring something to drink. We could help a young child who is too short to reach the water fountain get a drink of water. We could bring Mom a cool drink when she is hot and tired from mowing the lawn.

We can help conserve water by not wasting it. We should be careful not to pollute our water supplies. This will ensure that there will be enough water for everyone in the future.

How can we clothe the naked?

We often hear of the "street people" and how they have only the clothes they are wearing. Some of these people may be little children. We can help these people and others who don't have enough money to buy clothes by giving them the clothes that are too small for us. These clothes may be in good condition, and someone else can use them. We can ask our parents or teachers where our good, used clothes can be sent. When we help others, we are acting as Jesus acted. We are acting as images of God.

Jesus once told people, "Therefore I tell you, do not worry about your life, what you will eat [or drink], or about your body, what you will wear. Is not life more than food and the body more than clothing?" (Mt. 6:25). Jesus is telling us not to worry about fancy clothes. We should not be so worried about having the latest fashions. Instead, we should help those who are less fortunate. We should be happy with the things we have.

How can we visit those who are in prison?

Jesus' followers went to visit many people in prison. As followers of Jesus, we should want to do the same. There are many people in prison today. We can help by praying for them. Some people we know might not be in a prison with criminals, but they might feel as if they are prisoners in their own homes. Sometimes elderly people are not able to leave their houses. They can no longer drive, and they might not be able to take the public transportation. They might feel isolated because they no longer have many family members or friends around to help them. How can we help these people? Elderly people get lonely, and having someone to talk to will make them feel better. We can give them a call, write a letter, or visit them.

How can we shelter the homeless?

There are many people who do not have homes. We should be nice to people no matter where they live. We can pray for these people, that they may find a warm place for the night. If there is a shelter for the homeless in your area, you could donate a blanket or other items for these people. We can also help in other ways: by babysitting our neighbors' children after school until their parents come home from work, by helping our parents with cleaning the house, or by helping our neighbors around the yard. As images of God, we try to help others as Jesus did.

How can we visit the sick?

Jesus went around to all the towns and villages, teaching in their synagogues, proclaiming the gospel of the kingdom, and curing every disease and illness.
    —Matthew 9:35

Remember how Jesus always helped the sick? He talked to the lepers when everyone else avoided them. Is it always easy to visit the sick or to be around sick people? No, but if we want to act as Jesus did, we will help those who are sick.

Sometimes, when people get older, their health may not be good, and they might not be able to get out and see people. We can help by visiting these people and bringing them food or items they are not able to get. There are errands we could do for them, or we could just talk with them. Sometimes people in nursing homes have no one to visit them. We could send them cards or visit them as a class and put on a program for them. Perhaps we could go with a family member to visit a sick relative or friend.

What does it mean to bury the dead?

Jesus was very sad when His friend Lazarus died, and He tried to console the sisters of Lazarus, Martha and Mary. We should try to do the same when someone we know has lost a loved one. We should try to do what we can for them. We should pray for persons who have died and for their families. We could attend the funeral and send a card expressing our sorrow. We could put flowers on a grave of a relative or friend. When we do these things, we are acting as Mary did after Jesus died. We are acting as images of God.

The corporal works of mercy help people in their physical needs. The spiritual works of mercy help people in their spiritual needs. Jesus tried to meet not only the physical needs of people but their spiritual needs also. As images of God, we can do the same.

What does it mean to admonish the sinner?

"In just the same way, I tell you, there will be rejoicing among the angels of God over one sinner who repents."
    —Luke 15:10

Jesus came into the world to be our Savior and Redeemer. God the Father loved us so much that He gave His only Son to redeem us by dying on the Cross. When Jesus was on earth, He helped sinners by teaching them the truth and showing them how to act as images of God. Jesus told them what the right choices were, and He asked them not to sin.

Do you remember the story of the woman who had made a wrong choice, and how people were going to stone her? The people left after Jesus confronted them. When Jesus spoke to the woman, He did not get angry with her. Rather, Jesus told her that He did not condemn her, and He asked her not to make the same wrong choice again.

As images of God, we should imitate Jesus by teaching and showing others through our words and actions how to make right choices. If friends tell us about wrong choices they are thinking of making, we can tell them these choices are wrong ones. We should never tell people who are making wrong choices that they are bad persons. We can pray for them, and we can show them, by our example, how to make right choices. We can ask our friends to receive the sacrament of Reconciliation with us. It is an act of love to help others know what the right and wrong choices are. We can help each other make right choices by trying to be the best images of God we can be.

How can we instruct the ignorant?

"Just so, your light must shine before others, that they may see your good deeds and glorify your heavenly Father."
—Matthew 5:16

Jesus taught people about God by speaking to them about God, by telling the people parables, and by His loving example.

It is an act of love to help others learn the truths about God so that they can follow Him. We can do this by sharing our knowledge and love of God with others. We can help our friends with their religion homework. We can read a Bible story to our younger brothers and sisters and help them say their prayers. We can tell others what we believe about God. We can also be good examples to others by going to Mass on Sundays and Holy Days and participating in Mass by singing and saying the responses. We can be good listeners in our religion class and do our religion homework.

How can we counsel the doubtful?

He answered him, "Why do you ask me about the good? There is only One who is good. If you wish to enter into life, keep the commandments."
—Matthew 19:17

One time a man came up to Jesus and asked Him what he must do to have everlasting life. Jesus told him to follow the Ten Commandments, to sell all he had, and to follow Jesus. This man was not sure of all that he had to do to reach heaven. Jesus answered his questions and helped him to know how he could love and serve God. This was an act of love.

As images of God, we should imitate Jesus' act of love by helping others who are wondering how they can love and serve God better. We can do this by helping them understand the Ten Commandments and our Catholic beliefs and traditions better. Throughout our own lives, we should continue to learn more about our Catholic faith so we can help others be more certain about the Catholic faith.

How can we comfort the sorrowful?

"Come to me, all you who labor and are burdened, and I will give you rest."
    —Matthew 11:28

When Jesus was on earth, He helped and comforted people. For example, He comforted Martha and Mary when their brother Lazarus died, and Jesus shared their sorrow.

As images of God, we should imitate Jesus' act of love by giving comfort to others. We can try to cheer up a friend who is sad. We can listen in a careful and kind way when others share their troubles with us. Sometimes, when someone is very sad, we can help just by being with that person.

Jesus Himself experienced great sorrow. We remember how very, very sad Jesus was in the Garden of Gethsemane. He knew that soon He would be crucified. Jesus said to three of His Apostles, "My soul is sorrowful even to death" (Mt 26:38). Jesus experienced sorrow, so He knows how we feel when we are sad.

Sometimes there are things in our lives that make us sad. We can bring our sorrow to Jesus in prayer, and He will comfort us. This doesn't mean that Jesus will take away our sorrow, but He will be with us in our sorrow.

What does it mean to bear wrongs patiently?

"But I say to you, love your enemies, and pray for those who persecute you . . ."
    —Matthew 5:44

Jesus teaches us to love our enemies. Although Jesus had done nothing wrong, He was patient with those who arrested Him and took Him away. Jesus knew that people told lies about Him. He suffered and was crucified, but He didn't say a word. Jesus bore all these things for our sake. Jesus shows us how to be patient when others hurt us and even shows us that we should pray for those who hurt us.

We should imitate Jesus' acts of love by bearing wrongs patiently. For example, let's say someone draws on your desk at school. You are blamed for it, and you have no way to prove that you didn't draw on your desk. You end up having to stay after school to clean the drawing off your desk. If you accept this punishment quietly, without arguing, you are bearing a wrong patiently. You are suffering the consequences that the person who drew on your desk should suffer. This is an act of love.

What does it mean to forgive all injuries?

"If you forgive others their transgressions, your heavenly Father will forgive you. But if you do not forgive others, neither will your Father forgive your transgressions."
    —Matthew 6:14–15

Jesus forgave people's sins while He was on earth. He forgave the good thief and many others. Jesus even forgave the people who crucified Him when, as He was dying on the cross, He prayed: "Father, forgive them, they know not what they do" (Lk 23:34). Jesus shows us how to forgive others by the way He forgives others and us. We especially experience the forgiveness of Jesus in the sacrament of Reconciliation.

As images of God, we should forgive others as Jesus forgives us, even when they hurt us badly. Sometimes forgiving can be very hard to do. We should ask Jesus to help us follow His example and be forgiving. It is a great act of love to forgive a person who has hurt us.

What does it mean to pray for the living and the dead?

"Ask and it will be given to you; seek and you will find; knock and the door will be opened to you. For everyone who asks, receives; and the one who seeks, finds; and to the one who knocks, the door will be opened."
—Matthew 7:7–8

Jesus prayed to God the Father, and He taught us to do the same by teaching us the prayer "Our Father". At the Last Supper Jesus prayed for His Apostles and for all who believed and would believe in Him. He prayed that all may live with Him someday in heaven.

As images of God, we should pray for our families and friends that they may reach heaven someday. We should pray for the ill, the troubled, the unemployed, and all people. We should pray for those who have died that they may be with God in heaven. We should especially pray for those who are in purgatory. They cannot pray for themselves, so our prayers can help them reach heaven sooner. It is a loving act to pray for the living and the dead.

A STORY OF FAITH

We should imitate the loving acts of Jesus by practicing the corporal and spiritual works of mercy. One man who imitated Jesus' loving acts was Saint Vincent de Paul. As you read the story of Saint Vincent, see if you can pick out some of the corporal and spiritual works of mercy that he practiced.

Saint Vincent de Paul

SAINT Vincent was born on April 24, 1581, in the village of Pouy, France. His family were French peasants who made their living by farming.

Vincent had a natural gift for organizing things. Recognizing this gift, Vincent's cousin, Father Stephen de Paul, suggested that Vincent become a priest. Vincent, who was fourteen years old, agreed eagerly, because he didn't want to spend his life taking care of sheep and pigs. The priesthood offered him, a peasant, the chance to reach a high station in life. Vincent went to the city of Dax with his uncle and began his studies. At first he studied very hard just to please his family, but he continued his studies to please God.

Vincent's family made many sacrifices so that he could continue his education. Vincent's father even sold the family's precious oxen, which were of great importance on the farm. He used the money from the sale to pay for Vincent's education at the University of Toulouse. There Vincent studied theology and philosophy. When he saw his father sell the family's oxen, he remembered a time when he was in school at Dax. His father had come to see him at the school. But Vincent had hid from his father because he was ashamed of how his father looked. Vincent's small, thin father had come dressed in knee breeches and rough woolen socks. His shoes were worn out, and he limped as he hobbled along with his walking stick. Unable to find Vincent, his father had shuffled away, sad and disappointed. He never returned to the school again.

Vincent felt very ashamed of himself when he saw his father selling the precious oxen to help him. When his father gave him the money, Vincent didn't want to take it. But his father knew what had happened that day at the school in Dax. He gently told his son that although he was no saint, he was a good person and he would make a good priest. The next day Vincent left for school dressed in the new clothes his mother had made him. He had a pouch with an extra shirt and some food, and he had the money from the sale of the oxen. His parents hugged and kissed him, and Vincent began his journey to Toulouse.

In Toulouse, Vincent found a rather poor, cold place to stay. He studied very hard. His teachers were pleased with his work, and he did well. Vincent wrote to his family that winter to tell them how he was doing. When he received no reply, he wrote to a friend and asked if his friend had any news of Vincent's family. Vincent then learned that his father had become ill and had died. Although Vincent's father had made a will, stating that the family should continue to pay for Vincent's education, Vincent found work tutoring the sons of some wealthy families. The money he earned from this work paid for his education, so Vincent wrote to his family telling them that there was no need for them to continue to pay for his studies.

When Vincent was not quite twenty years old, he was ordained a priest. A period of great trial and hardship followed his ordination. He traveled to different cities, seeking a position, but had no success. When he was returning home by boat from Marseilles, pirates attacked and captured the boat. In the fight, Vincent was wounded in the leg by an arrow. This wound bothered him the rest of his life. The pirates took Vincent to a city called Tunis (in northern Africa) and sold him into slavery. Vincent suffered in slavery for two years, but he placed himself entirely in God's hands.

Vincent was rescued by a man named Gautier. Gautier had been a priest and had been captured by pirates and sold into slavery years before.

In order to buy his freedom, Gautier joined another religion. He owned a plantation, and he had married three women. One of Gautier's wives came to Vincent and asked him questions about the Catholic faith. Vincent answered all her questions. She, in turn, spoke with Gautier and told him he had made a great mistake in leaving the Catholic faith and the priesthood. Gautier knew that she was right. He went to Vincent, and the two escaped and returned to France.

After Vincent returned to France, he went to Paris. Having very little money and no immediate plans for his future, he needed a place to stay. Vincent and a judge rented a small room together.

Though often sick, Vincent spent many hours each day working in the charity hospital, which cared for those who could not afford to pay for health care. The conditions in the hospital were terrible. There was filth and stench everywhere. The food was poor, and the health care was inadequate. Four patients had to share one bed. The very, very ill and dying shared beds with those who were recovering. Many patients did not live.

It was there that Vincent came each day to tend to the patients' physical and spiritual needs. He was gentle and kind and did all he could to care for them.

One day, when Vincent was outside the hospital, he met Father Pierre de Bérulle. Father de Bérulle was interested in the care of the poor, and he had heard good things about Vincent. While Father de Bérulle and Vincent were talking, the judge with whom Vincent rented a room came and spoke to Vincent. The judge accused Vincent of stealing some of his money. Vincent denied this, but the judge didn't believe him. Father de Bérulle went on his way, and Vincent thought his chance of finding a position as a priest was lost. While the judge didn't have Vincent arrested, Vincent was labeled a thief, and rumor of the charge against him spread quickly through the city. Vincent carried this label for six months, until the real thief admitted to the crime.

Shortly after Vincent had met Father de Bérulle, and after the judge had accused Vincent of theft, Father de Bérulle found Vincent a position with Queen Mother Marguerite. Vincent's job was to distribute food and other items to the poor. During his work for the Queen Mother, he became a familiar figure around Paris, as he cared for the poor and the beggars.

Next, Father de Bérulle sent Vincent to a town called Clichy, where Vincent could continue to serve the poor. Vincent went there and found the church in great disrepair and the people extremely poor and uncaring. Vincent cleaned up the church with the help of some women. The men built more benches in the church, and the people filled the little church for Mass. The people loved Father Vincent. He taught their children about God and the Catholic faith. He celebrated the sacraments, he didn't scold, and he was never in too much of a hurry to sit and talk with those who were ill.

Then Vincent received a new assignment, tutoring the sons of the wealthy de Gondi family. The people of Clichy were very sad to see Vincent leave, and Vincent himself was filled with sorrow.

Vincent returned to Paris and began his work tutoring the de Gondi boys. The boys, however, were not interested in anything but sports and mischief. When Vincent wanted to leave his teaching position and return to work with the poor, Madame de Gondi suggested that Vincent work with the poor who lived in the villages belonging to the de Gondis. Vincent went through the villages and found conditions to be very poor. Madame de Gondi

herself went from hut to hut in the villages, teaching and nursing the people. Vincent followed her and administered the sacraments. This work went on for a year, and the physical and spiritual well-being of the people in these villages showed great improvement.

During this time, Vincent became well-known for his sermons, which were bringing many people back to the Church. One sermon brought so many people to confession that Vincent heard confessions the whole day. So great were the numbers of people coming to confession, that Madame de Gondi sent for additional priests to come and help Vincent.

Next, Father de Bérulle sent Vincent to a village called Châtillon-les-Dombes. When Vincent reached the village, he found the streets lined with taverns filled with people partying. The homes were boarded up, and the church was in very poor condition.

Father Vincent met a man named John Beynier, who had been drinking and was singing and walking down the road. Vincent rented a room from this man and began his work in the village. As in Clichy, Vincent cleaned the church with the help of some of the village women. The men came with hammers and nails to help with the repairs.

Soon people were going to Mass not only on Sundays but every day. Even the very wealthy baron of the village, who was a bully, came to see Vincent. The baron was so moved by his talks with Vincent that he sold everything he had and chose to follow the will of God. There was a very poor family that lived just outside the village. They were very near starvation. Vincent spoke to the village people at Mass and told them about the starving family. That evening, all the people, wealthy and poor alike, brought food to the family. Vincent knew that many poor families were in need. He decided to start an organization to handle the gathering and distribution of supplies to these poor families. In this way, everyone could eat, and nothing would be wasted.

This organization was the first Confraternity of Charity. John Beynier, the young man whom Vincent had met upon his arrival in the village, was put in charge of the confraternity. John had become a devout young Catholic. In the years to come, Vincent's confraternities would serve all of France, in peacetime and in war.

Soon, it was time for Vincent to leave the village of Châtillon and return to work for Madame de Gondi. Vincent became her spiritual director and continued his work with the poor in the villages. He began more Confraternities of Charity with the help of the men and women of the villages. The funds for supplies came from the wealthy. Vincent taught those who worked with the poor and sick that they must see the Person of Christ in the sick, so that whatever they did for the poor and sick, they would do it for Christ.

Vincent went to the prison and visited the men there. He found them chained to the walls. The chains were so short that the prisoners could not lie down to sleep. The men were dirty, with long beards. There were no windows, and the floor was covered with moldy straw. There were no proper records kept, showing the information on each prisoner and how long his sentence was. Therefore, prisoners were often kept in prison much longer than they should have been. Vincent spoke gently to each of the men and blessed them. He spoke to them about the suffering of Jesus and about the love Jesus had for each of them. After leaving the prison, Vincent went to see the person in charge and asked him to speak to the king about having proper records kept so that the prisoners would be released when their sentences were finished. Then Vincent cleaned and furnished a large house and made it into a hospital where the prisoners could be cared for. Throughout all France, Vincent visited the prisons and the ships' galleys (where prisoners were chained and where they worked rowing the big ships). He encouraged the prisoners to be patient and obedient.

Vincent began a group of priests called the Congregation of the Mission. The mission of these priests was to preach the Gospel to the poor and help to educate the clergy. They worked as missionaries to the small villages. He also helped to start the Sisters of Charity. With the help of these two groups, Vincent worked to improve the conditions of the charity hospital and to care for the patients there. He opened a seminary and conducted retreats for men interested in the priesthood. Vincent reformed prisons, and he opened orphanages, homes for the mentally ill, homes for the elderly, homes for the beggars, and hospitals for galley slaves.

During the civil war in France, Vincent and the Sisters of Charity ran soup kitchens to feed the poor. Vincent's charity kept thousands of people alive during this time. Vincent became ill during the war, and, even after the war ended, he never got back his health.

Near the end of his life, Vincent himself had to be cared for. His room was a bare little cell that couldn't be heated. Under doctor's orders, he was moved to a more comfortable room. On September 17, 1660, Vincent died in his sleep. He was canonized in 1737.

After reading the story about Saint Vincent de Paul, list examples that show how he practiced the corporal and spiritual works of mercy. Next to each example, indicate whether it is a corporal work of mercy (C) or a spiritual work of mercy (S).

- _____   C   S

- _____   C   S

- _____   C   S

- _____   C   S

- _____   C   S

- _____   C   S

- _____   C   S

11

Finding Happiness in Life

What are the beatitudes?
The beatitudes are the best ways that a person can think, feel, and act. By living the beatitudes we can be happy here on earth and someday with God in heaven.

Our life is a path towards paradise, where we will be loved and will love forever in a complete and perfect way. We are born only to go to paradise. The thought of paradise must make you strong against temptations. If you are united with Christ, you will triumph over every difficulty. I pray the Blessed Virgin to accompany you with her protection. Look upwards. Look up to Jesus and to those who really know Him, love Him and follow Him! Look to Jesus who is Truth, Love, the Example that illuminates, attracts and convinces! Every hope of yours is satisfied in Him! Jesus taught not only by word, but also by His actions in helping others. You have followed in His footsteps. He will surely reward you and fill you with His blessings.

POPE JOHN PAUL II

Vocabulary

meek: to be patient and gentle.
righteousness: acting according to God's will.
persecuted: mistreated and abused because of what one believes.

Jesus Teaches the People

One day Jesus went up a mountain. There He began to teach His disciples, saying:

> "Blessed are the poor in spirit,
>   for theirs is the kingdom of heaven.
> Blessed are they who mourn,
>   for they will be comforted.
> Blessed are the meek,
>   for they will inherit the land.
> Blessed are they who hunger and thirst for righteousness,
>   for they will be satisfied.
> Blessed are the merciful,
>   for they will be shown mercy.
> Blessed are the clean of heart,
>   for they will see God.
> Blessed are the peacemakers,
>   for they will be called children of God.
> Blessed are they who are persecuted for the sake of
>   righteousness,
>   for theirs is the kingdom of heaven."

—based on Matthew 5:1–10

Jesus went on to tell His disciples that they would be blessed when others would insult and persecute them because of their love of Christ. He told them they should rejoice and be glad, for their reward in heaven would be great.

Jesus gave us the beatitudes. They are the best attitudes we can have as images of God. They are the best ways to think, feel, and act. By living the beatitudes, we can find happiness in our everyday life amid joys and sorrows. By living the beatitudes, we can be happy here on earth and someday in heaven.

Blessed are the poor in spirit, for theirs is the kingdom of heaven.

Jesus was born in Bethlehem. He was not born in a hospital and wrapped in a blanket. Jesus was born in a stable and wrapped in swaddling clothes. Material things are not important to Jesus. People are always important to Him.

If we are to act as images of God and live this beatitude, we have to make God the most important Person in our lives. We should treat people as more important than things. We should not value new clothes, toys, and other things more than we value other people and God. We should think about people who have less than we do and share things with them. We should not ask our parents for everything we see on TV or in the stores. We shouldn't seek our friends because of what they have; for example, we shouldn't be friends with someone just because that person has a new bike or video games. We should think of all the things God has given us, through our parents, and try to be happy with what we have. Then we will be poor in spirit.

Blessed are they who mourn, for they will be comforted.

Do you remember the story of Lazarus (John 11:1–44)? What did Jesus do when Lazarus died? Jesus went to be with Mary and Martha when they were mourning their brother's death. He wanted to be with His friends even though it was dangerous for Him to go back to Judea, where Lazarus and his sisters lived.

After the Last Supper, Jesus went to the garden of Gethsemane. Jesus knew He was going to die. He was sad. He asked His friends to pray with Him. Jesus turned to God the Father for strength when He was sad (Mark 14:32–42).

When Jesus was carrying the Cross, how did Veronica help Him? Even though Veronica was sad, she tried to help Jesus. Veronica found a cloth and wiped the sweat and blood off Jesus' face.

When we are sad, we might think no one cares for us. We should try to remember that God always loves and cares for us. God is always there to listen to us. No matter how bad things may seem, God is always there. We should try also to console the people around us who are sad. If people are sad or troubled, we can listen to them and be friendly. We can let people know that we care by visiting with them. We should also pray for them.

Blessed are the meek,
for they will inherit the land.

When Jesus was on this earth, He was thoughtful of others. He cured the sick and helped those in trouble. Jesus always acted in a loving and caring manner. Jesus was meek.

Meek people never brag about themselves or think they are better than anyone else. A meek person lets others have a turn and tries to play fair all the time. A meek person never talks unkindly about other people. Meek people do not make fun of others or laugh at them when they make a mistake. If we act in a loving and caring manner, we are being meek, and we are acting as Jesus would.

Blessed are they who hunger and thirst for righteousness,
for they will be satisfied.

What does righteousness mean? It means acting according to God's will. What does it mean to be hungry and thirsty for righteousness? We know that if we are hungry or thirsty, we want something to eat or drink. To hunger and thirst for righteousness means that we want always to make the right choices. We want to do everything that God wants us to do.

What can we do in our daily lives to follow God and do His will? We can think about the Ten Commandments and try to follow them. We can listen in religion class and learn about our Faith. We should try to receive the sacraments of Reconciliation and Eucharist regularly. All of these things help us to know God and to do God's will.

Blessed are the merciful,
for they will be shown mercy.

Mercy means showing forgiveness. Jesus is merciful. Jesus forgives those who hurt Him. When Jesus was dying on the Cross, He even forgave those who had put Him there. He said, "Father, forgive them, they know not what they do" (Luke 23:34).

Jesus also showed mercy to the good thief when he was sorry for his wrong choices. Jesus promised the good thief that he would be with Jesus in heaven. Jesus shows us mercy. Every time we make a wrong choice, and we are sorry for it, Jesus will forgive us.

As images of God, we should forgive others the way Jesus does. How can we show mercy to others? If someone hurts your feelings by making fun of you, you should forgive that person. We can be kind to everyone, not just the people who like us. You should forgive a friend who lied and got you into trouble. You should not stay angry with your teacher when you have had to stay in for recess.

Jesus always forgives those who hurt Him, and we should do the same.

Blessed are the clean of heart,
for they will see God.

Jesus loves everyone, no matter who they are, what they have, or what they look like. Jesus always spoke to and helped the lepers (even though others avoided them). Jesus once stopped at a well to get a drink. There was a woman there who had made many wrong choices and was not living as an image of God. Jesus talked to her anyway. He loved the woman, as He loves everyone.

When we love as Jesus loves, we are acting as images of God in all that we think, do, and say. We treat others as images of God, no matter who they are, what they do, or what they look like. We should love them as God loves them.

When people are being mean toward us, it is hard to love them and not say mean things to them or about them. We should try to love them anyway and to do nice things for them.

Blessed are the peacemakers,
they will be called children of God.

What do you think a peacemaker is? A peacemaker is someone who helps people get along and who doesn't start fights. Jesus was a peacemaker. For example, Jesus stopped a fight between the Apostles and the soldiers who had come to arrest Him in the garden of Gethsemane. Peter had cut off an ear of one of the servants. Jesus told Peter to put away his sword. Jesus then healed the servant's ear (John 18:10–11).

A peacemaker is someone who treats everyone as an image of God. Through their actions, peacemakers show others how images of God should act. How can we be peacemakers? We can include everyone in our games. We should make sure everyone has a turn. We can make having fun the important thing in the game, not winning the game. At home, we can help Mom or Dad with the chores, without arguing whether it is our turn or not. We can be happy for a brother who got a new bike or sweater, instead of being envious. Like Jesus, we can be peacemakers and show our family and friends how to treat others as images of God.

Blessed are they who are persecuted for the sake of righteousness, for theirs is the kingdom of heaven.

What does "persecuted" mean? To persecute means to mistreat or abuse someone because of that person's beliefs. Many saints were persecuted because of their belief in God. Some saints even gave up their lives for Jesus. Can you think of any saints who were persecuted because they chose to believe in Jesus? These saints are examples of people who were persecuted for the sake of righteousness.

We know that we should do things that God wants us to do. For example, we should say our prayers before a meal, help our parents around the house (especially without being asked), go to church on Sunday, do our homework, and learn more about God. There are people who do not think these things are important. They might even make fun of us because we choose to do these things. Other people might try to talk us into not making the right choices. They will tell us that no one else is doing a certain thing, so why should we. They use peer pressure to try to convince us to change what we are doing. We can pray to God and ask Him to help us to be strong and to act as Jesus did.

A STORY OF FAITH

The beatitudes are simply ways of living our lives. They are the best ways of thinking, feeling, and acting in order to be happy here on earth and someday in heaven. One person who lived the beatitudes was a Mohawk Indian woman name Kateri Tekakwitha. When reading the following story, look for ways this woman lived the beatitudes.

Blessed Kateri Tekakwitha

TEKAKWITHA was born in 1656 near Auriesville, New York. Her father was chief of the Mohawk Indian tribe. Her mother, Kahenta, was from the Algonquin Indian tribe. Kahenta had married the Mohawk chief after she had been taken prisoner. Some Indian tribes were often at war with each other, and many prisoners were taken. The Mohawk Indians tortured and killed many of their prisoners. Other prisoners were made slaves.

Many of the Mohawks, including Tekakwitha's father, didn't like Christians or the missionary priests from France.

Tekakwitha's mother, however, was a devout Christian. She had been taught and baptized by the Jesuit priests from France. Kahenta taught Tekakwitha all she knew about God and tried to live a good Christian life. She hoped that one day Tekakwitha would be baptized.

Tekakwitha was a happy and pretty child. She listened to Kahenta and learned all that her mother taught her about God. Her mother was kind and gentle, and Tekakwitha learned to be kind and gentle, too. She enjoyed doing kind, little things for others.

When a smallpox epidemic hit the Mohawk village, many of the people became sick, including Tekakwitha and her family. Tekakwitha's parents and brother died, and though she survived, Tekakwitha suffered as a result of the smallpox. She was frail and weak, and her once beautiful face was scarred with pock marks. Her eyesight was blurred, and bright lights made her eyes sting.

Tekakwitha remembered all her mother had taught her about God, about Jesus and how He died for all people, and about Mary. Like her mother, Tekakwitha was quiet, gentle, and patient. Tekakwitha talked about God with her mother's friend, Anastasia, who was a Christian. Anastasia was a comfort to Tekakwitha, and the two often met and prayed together.

Tekakwitha's uncle was made the new Mohawk chief, and he and his wife adopted Tekakwitha. Tekakwitha worked hard to please them. She learned how to cook many different things made from corn. She made breads and puddings. She carried water from the stream. Because she could not see well, she didn't play games with the other children. Instead, she happily worked hard and became very good at making useful utensils and beautiful decorations.

From corn stalks she made such things as tubes for holding medicines, fish-line floats, and lotions. From corn she made dolls, bottles, trays, baskets, and sleeping mats. She made things out of corn cobs and made decorations out of kernels of corn. She made beautiful belts, moccasins, and ribbons decorated with beads she painted.

Again war broke out. The Mohawks were at war with the French Canadians and the Huron Indians. The French Canadian soldiers and the Huron Indians burned the Mohawk village and corn fields. The Mohawks escaped and hid in the forest. That winter was very hard on them. They had no homes to live in except makeshift shelters. Many died from the cold and from lack of food.

The Mohawks decided to sign a peace treaty with the French Canadians. The Mohawks built a new village and lived in peace with the French Canadians. The peace treaty called for the Mohawks to allow priests into their village. They also had to shelter and protect the priests. These rules didn't make Tekakwitha's uncle happy, because he didn't like Christians.

Tekakwitha's uncle gave her the responsibility of caring for the priests who came to the village. Although Tekakwitha was to wait on the priests, she was ordered by her uncle not to speak to them.

Tekakwitha wanted to receive the saving waters of Baptism and become a Christian. She watched the three priests as they went about their work. She admired the patience and love they showed the Indians. After three days, the priests had to travel on their way.

Two years later, one of the three priests returned. At that time, the Mohawks were at war with the Mohicans. The Mohawks had taken some

Mohican prisoners. The priest felt sick as the Mohawks tortured their Mohican prisoners. Only in Tekakwitha's eyes did the priest see compassion. The priest instructed and baptized the poor Mohican victims. The priest also baptized many of the Mohawk Indians, and he persuaded them to stop torturing their prisoners. Some of the Mohawks who were baptized went to live at a Christian mission known as the St. Francis Xavier Mission. The Indians called it the Praying Castle. Some of the Mohawks who left were friends of Tekakwitha. Anastasia was one of them.

When Tekakwitha was seventeen years old, her aunt and uncle wanted her to get married. If Tekakwitha married, her husband would hunt and provide food for her aunt and uncle. When Tekakwitha told them that she didn't want to marry, they became angry with her. They decided to trick her into getting married. They invited guests over, one of whom was a warrior who wanted to marry Tekakwitha. Tekakwitha's aunt and uncle had her dress in her nicest clothes and asked her to serve the guests. Tekakwitha's aunt asked her to serve the warrior some food in a special bowl. Tekakwitha recognized that the bowl was a ceremonial one and that she was being tricked into marrying the warrior. Tekakwitha dropped the bowl and ran out of her uncle's home, into the forest. When Tekakwitha returned, her aunt and uncle were very angry with her and treated her as a slave. Tekakwitha's uncle wouldn't even speak to her. This hurt Tekakwitha very much, because she loved her uncle. But even though her aunt and uncle mistreated her, Tekakwitha continued to be loving, gentle, and kind.

The warrior whom Tekakwitha had refused to marry was also very angry with her. One day, as she was busy working in her uncle's house, the warrior came and shouted at her. When she made no reply, he became even more angry and, taking his tomahawk, threatened to kill her. When the warrior raised his tomahawk to strike Tekakwitha, she said a prayer for him. He tried to kill her, but was not able to lower his arm to hurt her. Frightened, he stared at Tekakwitha, dropped his tomahawk, and ran from her uncle's house. After this incident, Tekakwitha's aunt and uncle no longer insisted that she marry.

Another priest came to the Mohawk village. His name was Father de Lamberville. The number of Mohawk Indians who became Christian increased every day. Many of them left to go and live at the mission.

One day, as Tekakwitha was working in the fields, she hurt her foot. Father de Lamberville went to see if he could help her. Tekakwitha told him of her great desire to be baptized and become a Christian. Listening to Tekakwitha, Father de Lamberville understood what a good and caring person she was. Father de Lamberville learned from other Indians in the village that Tekakwitha was a virtuous, caring, pure, and modest person.

Tekakwitha's uncle allowed Father de Lamberville to care for Tekakwitha's injured foot. This gave Tekakwitha the opportunity to learn more about God. Tekakwitha's uncle finally allowed Tekakwitha to be baptized, because he was afraid she would run away if he did not give his permission.

On Easter Sunday in 1675, Tekakwitha was baptized. She took the name of Kateri, which means Catherine. She was very happy.

Kateri would no longer work on Sundays, because it was the Lord's Day. She promised to work extra hard on the following day, but Kateri's aunt and uncle would not allow her to eat on Sundays if she would not work. So Kateri fasted on Sundays. She chose to fast on Wednesdays also.

After Kateri became a Christian, her aunt and uncle mistreated her, as did many of the other Indians in the village. Even the children threw rocks at Kateri. Kateri accepted this treatment with meekness and patience. She was loving and forgiving.

The harsh treatment Kateri received, along with the fasting, began to weaken her more and more. Father de Lamberville noticed her weakness and arranged for her to go to the St. Francis Xavier Mission. When her uncle was away from the village, some Indians from the mission near Montreal, Canada, took Kateri there. They traveled almost two hundred miles by canoe. Father de Lamberville sent along a note addressed to the priests at the mission in Montreal. He told them to guard and instruct Kateri well, because she was a special treasure.

In the mission, there were a chapel and many lodges for the Indians who lived there. Kateri was happy to be at the mission. Her friend Anastasia was there. Anastasia taught Kateri, as did Father Cholenc, one of the priests at the mission.

There were three Masses a day at the mission. The people would work in the fields after Mass. Three times during the day, a bell was rung, and the people stopped their work to pray. Every evening, the people were instructed by the priests.

The people in the mission noticed Kateri's holiness right away. She went to all three Masses and learned all she could about God. She had a devotion to Mary and prayed the Rosary. She visited the chapel whenever she could. She often prayed four to seven hours at a time. She prayed late into the night and was up very early in the morning. When she prayed, she thanked God for Baptism and for His love. Then she thought about Jesus, present in the Sacrament of the Altar. Then Kateri would talk to God and listen quietly for His answer. She asked God to bless her relatives with the gift of faith.

Kateri was friendly, happy, patient, and forgiving. She did all her tasks with great joy. Other Indians in the village tried to follow her example.

Kateri was allowed to make her First Communion early, because of her holiness. Usually, adults who were baptized had to wait two years before receiving their First Communion.

Of all the Indians in the mission, Kateri was the weakest physically, but the strongest in love for God and devotion to Him. She did many severe penances. Though she tried to do these in secret, the villagers became aware of what she was doing. She beat herself with rods, walked barefoot in the snow, and fasted often.

In addition, Kateri chose not to marry, which was very unusual for a Mohawk girl. Kateri wanted to make an official promise to God that she would not marry. Father Cholenc finally allowed her to make this promise, which she did with great happiness.

The penances Kateri chose to do began to weaken her. She became ill and suffered from dizzy spells and vomiting. Her friends wanted her to rest, but Kateri insisted she was well and continued to work. One friend noticed that Kateri looked more and more tired. She found that Kateri had been sleeping on branches of brambles and thorns instead of on soft, warm furs. She had also walked barefoot in the snow for an hour while praying.

When Father Cholenc learned of these things, he ordered her not to do any more penances.

Kateri's illness became worse, and she had to stay in bed. She had a constant fever and was always in great pain. She suffered from headaches and vomiting. But Kateri never complained. As she lay sick in bed, she spent some of her time teaching the children about God, and she helped those who were troubled.

During Holy Week, before Easter, Kateri asked Father Cholenc if she could fast, because she wanted to suffer something in honor of Christ's Passion. Father Cholenc told her that she was suffering enough already.

Kateri grew weaker and weaker. On Wednesday of Holy Week, April 17, 1680, Kateri died at the age of twenty-four, a slight smile on her face. The priests and villagers were gathered in her lodge. They knelt and prayed after her death. Fifteen minutes later, Father Cholenc looked at her. A miracle had happened. Kateri's face no longer had pock marks, her skin was healthy looking, and the smile on her face had increased.

Ten days after her burial, Kateri appeared in a vision to her friend Anastasia. In her hand, Kateri carried a cross. She showed Anastasia the cross and told her that the cross was the source of all her happiness during her life. Kateri asked Anastasia to make it hers also. Then Kateri disappeared.

In a vision to another person, Kateri said that the mission chapel would be destroyed. That August, a hurricane hit the mission, and the chapel was destroyed by the wind. The priests had prayed at Kateri's grave before the hurricane. Normally the debris would have hurt the priests or killed them. Instead, one priest was only slightly injured, and the other two were un-harmed. The priests thought it was Kateri's prayers that had protected them.

A year after Kateri's death, Father Cholenc heard of a Frenchman who was dying of lung cancer. Father Cholenc placed the man under Kateri's protection, and the man was cured of his cancer.

Many French and Indians begged Kateri's aid, and many cures were reported.

Kateri has not yet been declared a saint, but she lived a very holy life. We can see in the story of her life how she lived the beatitudes. Though she suffered a great deal, she found happiness in her love of God. We celebrate a feast day in her honor on July 14.

To help us live the beatitudes, we can say the following prayer every morning.

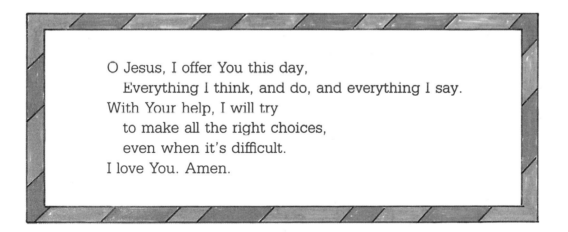

O Jesus, I offer You this day,
    Everything I think, and do, and everything I say.
With Your help, I will try
    to make all the right choices,
    even when it's difficult.
I love You. Amen.

Unit 4

Jesus
Is with Us

12

The Church Guides Us

Who remains with us through the Church today?
Jesus.

Who is the leader of the Church on earth?
The Pope.

Who carries on the work Jesus gave the Apostles?
The Pope and bishops.

Who are the helpers to the bishops?
The priests.

Who does the work of the Church?
The Pope, bishops, priests, deacons, all members of the Church.

Vocabulary

Pope: the person who takes Peter's place and is the leader of the Catholic Church on earth.

bishops: the men who today teach the people how to act as images of God the way the Apostles did.

ordained priests: the men who have answered God's call and have been ordained to offer their lives to Him and be helpers to the bishops.

lay people: the non-ordained, baptized members of the Church who love and serve the Lord in their jobs and families.

missionaries: persons who go to other countries (or to a different part of their own country) to love and serve God and others.

diocese: the people and territory under the care of a bishop.

You know that Jesus chose the twelve Apostles and gave them alone His powers for the carrying out of their mission: To announce the Truth, to save and sanctify souls, to guide the Church.

He set Peter at the head of the Twelve, as the foundation of the Church and the universal pastor of all souls, with the duty of "strengthening his brothers".

He has from the Lord special help in order not to make a mistake about faith and morality.

The mission and the powers of the Apostles passed to the bishops.

The mission and the powers of Peter passed to the Pope, that is, to the Bishop of Rome, his successor.

You see how, in the will and plan of Jesus, the Church is one body, perfectly united and linked together: The bishops form a unity with Peter, that is, with the Pope, as their head.

POPE JOHN PAUL II

The Holy Spirit Helps the Apostles

We know that Jesus, God the Son, came to show us who we are and how we should act as images of God. Jesus also came to return God's love and to help us return God's love. We know that Jesus died for us, that He has risen, and that He is now in heaven. However, Jesus did not abandon us. He had the Apostles, with the help of the Holy Spirit, carry on His work.

After Jesus rose from the dead on Easter Sunday, He met many times with the Apostles. Before He ascended into heaven, Jesus promised the Apostles that He would send the Holy Spirit to them. Jesus asked the Apostles to stay in Jerusalem until this happened. Jesus told them to wait for "the promise of the Father about which you have heard me speak; for John baptized with water, but in a few days you will be baptized with the Holy Spirit". Jesus then ascended into heaven, and the Apostles stayed together in a home in Jerusalem.

One day, when the Apostles were all together, they heard a noise. It was like the sound of a strong wind. This sound filled the house. Then there appeared to the Apostles tongues of fire, which parted and came to rest on each one of them. They were all filled with the Holy Spirit and began to speak in different languages.

A large crowd gathered to listen to the Apostles. They were astounded! Although these people were from many different countries and spoke different languages, they heard the Apostles speaking in their own languages.

The Apostles baptized many people that day. The Apostles, with the help of the Holy Spirit, taught the early Christians who they were and how they should act as images of God.

—based on Acts 1:1–5, 2:1–41

Pope John Paul II has visited numerous countries to spread Jesus' message. We have read many of his thoughts at the beginning of some of the lessons in this book. Let's read about the life of Pope John Paul II before he became Pope.

Pope John Paul II—Karol Wojtyla

KAROL WOJTYLA was born on May 18, 1920, in Wadowice, Poland. He had one brother, Edmund, who was much older than he. Karol's mother died when he was only nine years old. Then, when Karol was twelve years old, his brother became very sick and died.

As he was growing up, Karol enjoyed playing different sports. He especially liked to ski in the winter months. He also liked to take long walks in the evening with his father.

Karol was an excellent student who never got in trouble for bad behavior or poor grades. Growing up, Karol never thought of becoming a priest. His dream was to attend a university to study literature and to become an actor. In 1938, when he was eighteen, Karol graduated from high school. He and his father moved to the city of Cracow so that Karol could attend the Jagiellonian University.

During his free time, Karol enjoyed exploring the city of Cracow, its castles, churches, and monasteries. He would spend many hours praying in church. He also enjoyed reading poetry and performing in the theater.

During this time, Adolf Hitler was the leader of the Nazi party of Germany. His dream was to take over all the countries in Europe. In 1939, Hitler and his army attacked and took over Poland. The Nazis wanted to take away the freedom of the Polish people. One way they did so was by preventing the Polish people from getting an education. Hitler's soldiers arrested many of the university professors. The Jagiellonian University had to close. But Karol and his fellow students wanted to continue their education, so they would meet secretly, at night, even though they knew they could be arrested at any time.

Karol had to find a job. Those who had no job were sent to Germany to work in a labor camp. He found work in a limestone quarry. At the quarry, the workers hammered out stones from the hard ground and then loaded the stones into wagons.

Food was hard to find. Somehow Karol was always able to find something to bring home to share with his father. Unfortunately, one day Karol came home to find his father dead. He felt very alone, and he moved into a friend's apartment.

Around this time, he began to study theology. He did not tell anyone else what he was doing. He was beginning to think about becoming a priest.

Karol and his friends did not want Polish culture to die, so they began an underground theater (done secretly so the Nazis would not find out). If they had been caught, they would have been shot or sent to prison. Karol wrote many of the poems that were read and plays that were performed by the theater group.

Hitler did not like a lot of people, especially Jews. He ordered that all Jews be arrested. Those arrested were sent to prison or were killed. Karol knew it wasn't right to imprison or to kill the Jews. Karol helped hide Jews until they could be given safe passage out of the country. If Karol had been caught helping the Jews escape, the Nazis would certainly have killed him. The Nazis tried to prevent people from practicing their religion. Many Catholics were arrested, including many bishops, priests, sisters, and students. Life was becoming very dangerous for Karol.

In Cracow, Archbishop Sapieha decided to hide the young men who were studying to become priests. He lived in an old palace. The students lived in passageways under the palace. So Karol spent the rest of the war hiding in the archbishop's house. Karol and his fellow students were able to continue their studies secretly and safely. After the war, Karol continued his studies to become a priest. Archbishop Sapieha, now a cardinal, ordained Karol on November 1, 1946. Cardinal Sapieha recognized that Father Karol Wojtyla had special talents, so he sent him to Rome to study further.

When Father Wojtyla came back to Poland, he worked in a few poor parishes. He always dressed and ate the same way his parishioners did. Even though he could have worn nice clothes, he never wanted to. At the same time, he was able to continue his studies at the Jagiellonian University, which had reopened after the war.

Although Hitler and the Nazis had lost the war, the Polish people did not regain their religious freedom. Now the Communists ruled the country, and they tried to discourage all religious practices. The Communists tried to silence the Catholics by putting many of the priests and bishops in prison. Even a cardinal, Cardinal Wyszynski, was placed under arrest for three years. In addition, in 1954, the Communist government closed the theology department at the Jagiellonian University.

Fortunately, the Catholics were able to establish a Catholic University in Lublin. Here, Father Wojtyla gave many lectures. He was one of the students' favorite teachers. He was very enthusiastic and interesting.

Father Wojtyla enjoyed teaching very much. When he became a bishop in 1958, he was very busy. He loved teaching and did not want to give it up. So he combined his love of the outdoors with his teaching. He would take his students up to the mountains and lecture while they were hiking. Bishop Wojtyla continued to write many books, plays, poems, and articles during this time.

The Communist government would not allow any new churches to be built, but that didn't stop Karol Wojtyla. He often spoke out against the

Communist government. He and the people marched in protest and demanded that a new church be built near Cracow. Finally, the government allowed it to be built.

In May 1967, Bishop Wojtyla became a cardinal. As a cardinal, he traveled and spoke at many religious meetings all over the world. He traveled to the United States often.

Cardinal Wojtyla never wanted anyone to serve him or show him any special treatment. He enjoyed visiting with people, especially children. He had a great sense of humor. Even though he was very busy, he spent a lot of time in his chapel, praying.

When Pope John Paul I died suddenly, after only 33 days as Pope, Cardinal Wojtyla flew to Rome. Other cardinals, from all over the world, also came to Rome for the funeral. After the funeral, the cardinals met to elect a new Pope. This meeting is called a conclave; it is held in the Sistine Chapel, in Rome. Once a conclave begins, no one can enter or leave. The cardinals are not allowed any contact with the outside world.

The cardinals discussed who should be the next Pope. Then each one wrote on a card the name of the person whom he wanted to be Pope. When the ballots were counted, the cardinals let the outside world know the result. (A candidate needs at least 75 votes to be elected Pope.) The world watched the stovepipe chimney on the roof of the Sistine Chapel. If a new Pope had been elected, they would see white smoke. If no one had received at least 75 votes, there would be black smoke. After the eighth ballot, the crowd that had gathered outside saw white smoke! Karol Wojtyla had been elected. He was the first non-Italian Pope in more than four hundred years.

The people of Poland were very proud that someone from their country had been elected Pope. However, the Communist government was not excited. In fact, the government would not allow some of the Pope's friends to leave the country in order to attend Karol Wojtyla's installation Mass. Karol Wojtyla decided to take as his papal name John Paul II. He travels all around the world. Pope John Paul II continues to spread the good news of Jesus.

Saint John Neumann

JOHN NEUMANN was born March 28, 1811, in Prachatitz, Bohemia, which is now part of Czechoslovakia. His family were devout Catholics and were well known in the village. He had two sisters and one brother. John's father was a stocking maker. The money John's father earned from the business allowed the family to live a comfortable life. John's father, who had served on the town council and as overseer of the poor, was known as a kind and a just man.

The Neumann home was a prayerful one. John's mother, a deeply religious woman, attended Mass every day, and John often went with her.

John had a quick mind for study, he enjoyed reading a great deal, and he had the rare talent of learning many different languages. When the time came for John to decide what kind of work he wanted to do in his life, he thought about becoming a priest. There were so many young men who wanted to join the seminary in the city of Prague that John worried about being accepted. John's mother encouraged him to apply, and John was accepted with no problem.

John began his studies at the diocesan seminary in the town of Budweis and continued his studies at the Charles Ferdinand University in Prague. There John was known for his sound reasoning, his thinking, and his holiness. People noticed that John had a great devotion to God and love for Him.

The diocese of Budweis had more priests than it needed, so it was not ordaining any new priests. John had heard reports of a very great need for priests in the United States. He decided to become a missionary priest there. He tried to contact the Catholic Church in the United States to see if he would be accepted as a priest there. Even though he was not yet ordained and did not know if he had been accepted as a priest in the United States, John left his country and family and sailed to New York. John trusted that this was what God wanted him to do.

While traveling to the United States on board the ship *Europa*, John wrote in his diary every evening. Writing in his diary was a nightly habit that John had begun when he was in the seminary. In it he recorded his struggles, victories, and defeats as he sought perfection. It showed John's great desire to know God and to do His will. John had a strong sense of being inadequate, and he felt a great dependence on God. The diary was a careful record of the distress and uncertainty he felt in his search to know God and to follow His will.

It took forty days for the *Europa* to reach the United States, and because it was packed with all the passengers it could hold, there was very little privacy for anyone on board.

John was a small, stockily built man, 5 feet 4 inches tall. He was very shy, reserved, studious, prayerful, and thoughtful. Some of the ill-mannered passengers made fun of him. John wrote in his diary that God had given him an opportunity to practice humility in the face of contempt and insults from some of his fellow travelers. John bore the insults patiently. He was lonely for companionship, but he seemed unable to make friends with his fellow passengers.

John had decided in his seminary days never to waste a minute, so he spent his time on board ship reading. He especially enjoyed reading a book by Saint Francis de Sales and another book called *The Imitation of Christ*. He read them when he could find a little peace and quiet. He also read a letter from Saint Francis Xavier, a missionary, to Saint Ignatius Loyola. The letter was written in Spanish. (John spoke Latin, Greek, and six other languages.)

John Neumann and his fellow passengers found the trip tiring, and they were anxious for it to end. They had been at sea through good and bad weather for almost forty days. Food supplies were low, and the drinking water had worms in it and had a terrible odor. Some passengers became ill; others quarreled. Everyone felt the strain of the long voyage. Finally, one rainy morning in May, a crew member called out from his lookout position that he could see land. All the passengers shouted for joy and gathered at the railing of the ship to look at their new country.

John Neumann landed in New York on May 28, 1836, the feast of Corpus Christi. John carried his few belongings and his treasured books and left the ship. His clothes were shabby, his shoes were worn, and he had only a dollar left in his pocket. John thanked God for his safe voyage to the United States and wondered what his future would be.

The following day, John went to the cathedral in New York. There, he learned that the bishop had been told about John's desire to be a priest in the United States. John had been accepted. There was a great need for priests in the New York diocese, which at that time included all of the state of New York and part of New Jersey. Two hundred thousand people were members of the Catholic Church in the New York diocese, but there were only 36 priests. John's arrival had been eagerly awaited, and he was warmly welcomed.

John was ordained a priest three weeks after his arrival in New York. During those three weeks, he helped to prepare thirty children for First Communion. John loved children and enjoyed teaching them their catechism. After his ordination, at his first Mass, John gave First Holy Communion to those thirty children he had taught. John also made a promise to pray the Rosary every day of his life and to ask Mary's help in all that he did.

At this time, immigrants from different countries of Europe were coming to the United States, and many settled in New York. They came from Germany, from Italy, from Ireland, or from other countries. Most of these people didn't speak English. Their life in the United States was very difficult. They had to clear the land of rocks, shrubs, and trees so that they could farm. They had to build some sort of home, which usually had a dirt floor. Many of them lacked money and food.

Father Neumann spent a short time in Rochester, New York, and then went on to Williamsville, near Buffalo, New York, where he served as priest for Williamsville and the surrounding area. There were four hundred Catholic families in this area of more than nine hundred square miles. Father Neumann traveled by foot from village to village, carrying, in a pack on his back, his vestments and everything he needed to say Mass and celebrate the sacraments. The walking was difficult because the land was covered with many forests and swamps. Father Neumann traveled this area whether it was summer or mid-winter. He carried out his duties as a priest in the different villages. He baptized the people, heard their confessions, married them, taught them their catechism, and said Mass. He also taught school twice a day when he was in Williamsville.

On one of his journeys, Father Neumann stopped to rest because his feet had become covered with painful blisters. Soon after he sat down, he was surrounded by Indians. He had heard of Indians' robbing travelers and expected that he would be robbed also. But the Indians had a great respect for this priest. Seeing his blistered feet, they carried him on a blanket to the next village.

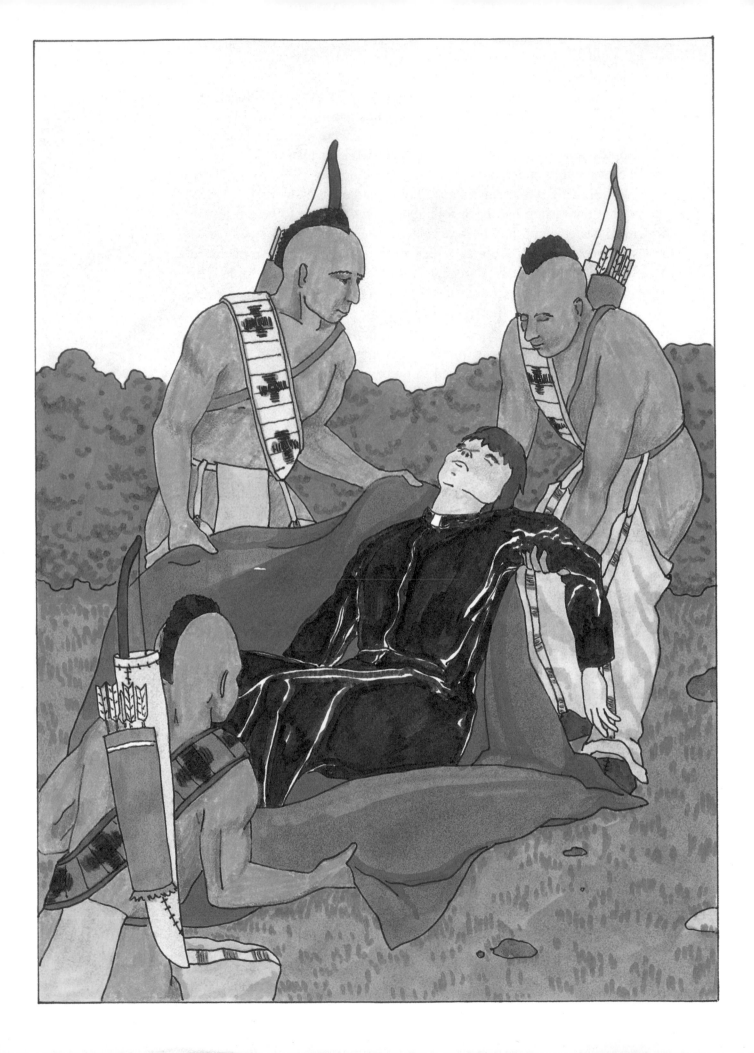

Father Neumann spent four years serving the people in the Williamsville area—helping them build churches and setting up schools wherever he could. In the summer of 1840, Father Neumann was completely worn out and exhausted from the hard work and self-sacrifice, and he became seriously ill. It took three months of rest and proper food before he regained his health. While recovering, he decided to join the Redemptorist Order of priests. After two years of preparation, he made his vows and became a priest-member of the Congregation of the Most Holy Redeemer (the Redemptorists).

Returning to the missionary territory as a Redemptorist priest, Father Neumann served the German-speaking Catholics in Baltimore. In 1844, he became the pastor of St. Philomena's Church in Pittsburgh. The church was only partially built, and there was a debt of seventeen thousand dollars. Father Neumann started a Church Building Society. He asked each parishioner to give five cents a week (a large amount of money at that time). The parishioners gave gladly, even though they were very poor. On the feast of the Holy Rosary in October 1846, after their many months of struggling to pay for its completion, the beautiful Gothic-style church was dedicated. The people were filled with joy at what they had accomplished through their efforts and sacrifices.

In addition to his priestly duties, Father Neumann found time to write a catechism and a Bible history for instructing the hundreds of children in the three schools under his direction.

Once again, Father Neumann became very ill after completely wearing himself out caring for the people in his parish. After his recovery, at the age of thirty-five, he was appointed the Superior of the Redemptorist Order in the United States. He was sent to St. Alphonsus parish in Baltimore. Father Neumann helped a group of religious sisters—of the School Sisters of Notre Dame—to set up a mother house in Baltimore. He asked them to teach at St. Alphonsus parish, and they did. Father Neumann often visited the classrooms to see how the children were doing. He had a special gift for teaching children, and he formed a close bond with them. The children often said that Father Neumann looked right into their hearts. One of the sisters, who had a habit of raising her voice and losing her patience while teaching, learned to correct the fault after Father Neumann surprised her several times: he entered the room so quietly that she hadn't noticed he was there until he greeted her.

There was a boy in the school who often caused trouble for his father and for his teachers. The teachers asked Father Neumann to have the boy dismissed, for they could do nothing with him. Father Neumann decided, instead, to spend one hour each day teaching the boy. Under Father Neumann's guidance, the boy's behavior and attitude improved so much that his father and his teachers were amazed.

Father Neumann had a great interest in setting up Catholic parochial schools. With the help of the School Sisters of Notre Dame, Catholic parochial schools were set up in Philadelphia, Pittsburgh, and Buffalo. The sisters also taught in the school of the Most Holy Redeemer in New York City.

Near the end of the year 1851, Bishop Kenrick, a long-time friend of Father Neumann, became archbishop of Baltimore. He had served as bishop of Philadelphia for twenty years, and it was his privilege to name three priests who were qualified to take his place as bishop of Philadelphia. Of the three priests he named, Father Neumann was the one he thought could best take his place. Many bishops were in favor of Father Neumann's appointment, because they knew he could serve and care for the poor, whom he knew and understood. Other bishops did not think Father Neumann was the right choice to serve as bishop for the wealthy, sophisticated people of Philadelphia.

The Pope made the final decision. He chose Father Neumann to be the new bishop of Philadelphia. In 1852, at age forty-one, Father Neumann was consecrated bishop of Philadelphia. Bishop Neumann didn't want the usual big celebration in his honor. Instead, the people in charge of welcoming the new bishop to Philadelphia promised to build a new school in his honor. This sign of welcome made him very happy.

Many wealthy people lived in Philadelphia. Their lives were much easier than the lives of the poor people who also lived there. Bishop Neumann gave most of his attention to the poor. In addition to dealing with the spiritual needs of the people, he had to deal also with the financial matters of the diocese. Although the Philadelphia diocese, like many other dioceses, was in debt, Bishop Neumann chose to spend money on building churches. He regarded these new churches as necessary to meet the spiritual needs of the immigrants coming to the United States.

As one of his duties, Bishop Neumann made occasional visits to the distant and remote areas of his diocese. On these visits he traveled by foot, train, or stagecoach—whatever means of travel was necessary to get him to the out-of-the-way places. He enjoyed these visits because he was bringing God's forgiveness, love, and charity to the people. In these small parishes Bishop Neumann celebrated Mass, heard confessions, visited the sick, celebrated Confirmation, and met with Catholics who were no longer practicing their religion. He loved the people, and they loved him. These visits reminded the bishop of the years when he had been a missionary priest in New York.

Bishop Neumann attended the First Plenary Council of Baltimore. This council was a meeting of the bishops in the United States. The council made decisions and plans that affected the Catholic Church in the United States for many years. Bishop Neumann was on a committee that dealt with parish schools. The committee urged pastors to open Catholic parochial schools in their parishes, even though they could not get help from the government. The council also approved a catechism written by Bishop Neumann that was used by German parishes.

Bishop Neumann organized a central board of education in his diocese to establish Catholic parochial schools. The board members included himself,

pastors, and laymen. Bishop Neumann hoped to have a Catholic parochial school in every parish, and over the years he was successful. The current Catholic parochial school system in the United States grew out of the central board of education begun by Bishop Neumann. The opening of Catholic parochial schools was a major concern to him, and he was pleased to see the number of Catholic parochial schools increase.

Although extremely busy with all his duties, Bishop Neumann always had time for those who came to see him and to bring their concerns to him. Many of these people were poor. He helped them all, giving them money and even, on occasion, giving away his own clothes.

Bishop Neumann wanted to begin a Forty Hours Devotion to Jesus in the Blessed Sacrament (Holy Eucharist). This devotion requires that the Blessed Sacrament be exposed for adoration for forty consecutive hours, even during the night. There was some prejudice against Catholics at this time, and Bishop Neumann was concerned about the safety of the Blessed Sacrament and about the possibility of people disrupting the devotion. However, he believed that God wanted this devotion, so he carried out his plan. Forty Hours Devotion was observed throughout the Philadelphia diocese all year round—first in one parish and then in another.

In 1854, Bishop Neumann was invited to Rome to be present as the Church declared her teaching on the Immaculate Conception of the Blessed Virgin Mary: that Mary was kept free of original sin; that she was conceived and born with grace. After the trip to Rome for this special occasion, Bishop Neumann visited his family, whom he hadn't seen in 18 years. He was very happy to see his father again. (His mother had died while he was in the United States.)

Then Bishop Neumann returned to Philadelphia and his duties. He still loved most the duty of visiting the remote parishes of his diocese. He even traveled a whole day in the Allegheny Mountains to confirm one boy. In one town where he heard confessions, he found that many people spoke only Gaelic (a language of Ireland). When he returned to Philadelphia, Bishop Neumann studied Gaelic; and the next time he went to that town, he heard confessions in Gaelic and in English. The people were very grateful to him.

Bishop Neumann was loved by the people in his diocese, especially the poor. He visited, cared for, and helped them whenever he could. Archbishop Kenrick said that Bishop Neumann was a father to the poor, the humble, and the lowly.

In 1857, a priest named James Frederick Wood was consecrated bishop to share the duties of the diocese of Philadelphia with Bishop Neumann. Bishop Wood had been in banking and was especially helpful in financial matters. The arrangement of sharing the diocesan duties worked out quite well.

On January 5, 1860, as Bishop Neumann was out taking care of some errands, he fell to the ground on a street in Philadelphia. Two strangers carried him into a home nearby. He died there several minutes later.

At his funeral, the rich and the poor, the young and the old, showered honor and praise upon Bishop Neumann. Archbishop Kenrick remarked in his homily at the funeral Mass that Bishop Neumann had been a good and devoted shepherd, living only for his flock.

Bishop John Neumann's body was entombed in the sanctuary vault of St. Peter's chapel. Many people came to the tomb, to petition John Neumann for help in their lives. They asked him to bring their petitions before the throne of God. Stories were told of the miracles that had taken place after petitions had been made to Bishop Neumann. There was a man who had been seriously injured in a car accident and whose condition was considered hopeless. His mother obtained a piece of Bishop Neumann's cassock and placed it on her son. He recovered completely from his injuries. An eleven-year-old girl who was dying prayed to Bishop Neumann for a cure. The next morning the doctor found her completely cured. A nineteen-year-old boy from New Jersey who suffered from cancer of the leg, jaw, and lungs was completely cured after his family prayed to Bishop Neumann for his recovery.

On June 19, 1977, Pope Paul VI declared Bishop John Neumann a saint. Bishop Neumann truly carried on the work that Jesus gave the Apostles, by teaching and caring for the people of his time.

When we were baptized, we became members of the Catholic Church. Each of us is joined with Jesus Christ, with the Holy Spirit, and with other Catholics. Together we are the Church. Jesus is the leader of the Church. The Holy Spirit guides the Church. The Pope is the leader of the Church on earth. The Pope and bishops carry on the work Jesus gave the Apostles. The Church guides us and helps us to act as images of God so that one day we may live in heaven. Jesus said, "I am with you always, until the end of the age" (Matthew 28:20). Jesus remains with us through the Church.

As members of the Church we are called to love and serve God and others. We should love and serve God. We should care for, love, and help other members of the Church—in our community, in other states, and in other countries. We should act as images of God, and we should help other members of the Church to grow in the love of God. When we do these things, we are doing the work of the Church.

The Church needs you, the world needs you, because it needs Christ, and you belong to Christ. Help by your words, and, above all, by the example of your lives, to spread the Gospel. You do this by praying, and by being just and truthful and pure. Dear young people: by a real Christian life, by the practice of your religion you are called to give witness to your faith. And because actions speak louder than words, you are called to proclaim, by the conduct of your daily lives that you really do believe that Jesus Christ is Lord!
—Pope John Paul II

Ministries in the Church

We all love and serve God and others in different ways.

The Pope, bishops, priests, and deacons devote their entire lives to God. They love and serve God and others. The Pope and the bishops in union with him are guided by the Holy Spirit and teach us the same things Jesus taught. They celebrate the sacraments. They teach us, guide us, and help us to grow in love of God. The priests and deacons help the bishops guide and care for us.

Religious brothers and sisters also devote their entire lives to God. They love and serve God and others. They do many acts of love, including teaching in schools, caring for the sick, and visiting the prisons.

Some Popes, bishops, priests, brothers, and sisters are well-known for their lives of love and service to God and others.

Pope John Paul II has traveled to many countries throughout the world, loving and caring for the people and teaching them about God.

Saint John Neumann came to the United States from Europe to become a missionary priest and later a bishop. He was devoted to loving, caring for, and teaching the people.

Father Damien de Veuster was a missionary priest who left his home in Europe and went to the Hawaiian Islands. There he built four chapels, but he is best known for his work with the lepers on the island of Molokai. Father Damien cared for the lepers and worked to provide them with proper housing, medical care, and employment. Father Damien continued his work even after he became ill with the painful disease of leprosy. He died on April 15, 1889.

Mother Teresa of Calcutta started a new religious order called the Missionaries of Charity. Many men and women have become priests, brothers, and sisters in this order. Mother Teresa and the Missionaries of Charity love, serve, and care for the poor in India and other countries.

Some lay people also are well known for their love and service to God and others.

Saint Thomas More lived many years ago in England. He was married and had four children. Thomas became Lord Chancellor of England, a high-ranking government office. He was wise and just in performing his duties. Though he was busy with government affairs, he spent time with his family, leading them in prayer and reading the Scriptures. Henry VIII, King of England at that time, decided to divorce his wife, Catherine, so he could marry another woman. Thomas knew that this would be wrong and disapproved of the divorce so much that he resigned his position as chancellor. After he resigned, Thomas spent several years writing and living quietly with his family. Then, Thomas was asked to acknowledge King Henry VIII as head of the Church in England. Thomas refused to do so and, after fifteen months of imprisonment, was beheaded. He died as a martyr defending the Catholic faith. He was declared a saint in 1935. His feast day is June 22.

Tom Dooley used his talents as a doctor to love and serve God and others by providing medical care for the people of Viet Nam and Laos. Tom set up hospitals and loved and cared for the people in these two countries. Tom's faith helped him with his work. He went to daily Mass and prayed the Rosary often. He became ill with cancer, but he continued to work in Laos until his illness forced him to return to the United States. He died at the age of thirty-four.

Dorothy Day became a Catholic at the age of thirty. She then spent many years loving and serving God and others. Dorothy opened hospitality houses where the poor could come for food, shelter, and clothing. She and those who worked with her lived in poverty, also. They lived in the hospitality houses. Dorothy and her helpers published a paper called *The Catholic Worker*, which sold for one penny a copy. They used this money, along with charitable donations, to support their work. Life in the hospitality houses was difficult. It was a life of poverty and hard work. More and more people came to be fed, sheltered, and clothed. Eventually about forty hospitality houses were opened. Dorothy became a woman of prayer, and it was her love for God and her faith in Him that enabled her to continue the work she had started. This work continues today.

Fill in the information on this chart.

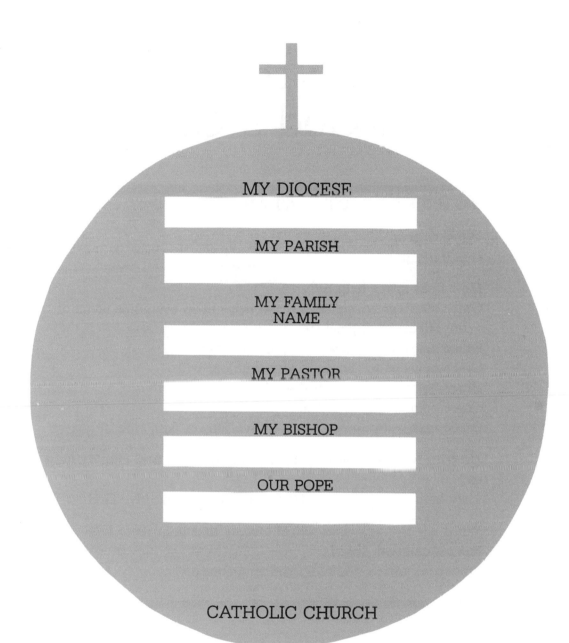

MY DIOCESE

MY PARISH

MY FAMILY
NAME

MY PASTOR

MY BISHOP

OUR POPE

CATHOLIC CHURCH

WE ARE MEMBERS OF THE CATHOLIC CHURCH

WE ARE MEMBERS OF THE WORLDWIDE CATHOLIC COMMUNITY

13

With the Help of God's Grace

What is grace?
God's life in us.

How does grace help us?
Grace takes away original sin and helps us to overcome some of the effects of original sin.
Grace helps us to know the truth about God.
Grace helps us to choose to love with our wills.
Grace helps us to use self-discipline.
Grace helps us to act as images of God.
Grace makes it possible for us to live forever with God in heaven.

How do the theological virtues of faith, hope, and charity help us?
They help us to believe in God, trust in God, and love God.

What are the principal moral virtues that help us to lead moral, or good, lives?
Prudence, justice, fortitude, and temperance.

Vocabulary

grace: God's life in us.
theological virtues: the supernatural powers that help us to believe in God (faith), to trust in Him (hope), and to love Him (charity).
moral virtues: the supernatural powers that help us to lead moral, or good, lives.

A STORY OF FAITH

Saul of Tarsus

ONE man who received God's grace was Saul of Tarsus, a Jew. Saul persecuted Jesus' followers after Jesus ascended into heaven and after the Holy Spirit came to the Apostles. Saul went on a journey to the city of Damascus. He intended to find the followers of Jesus who were there and bring them back to Jerusalem in chains. On the way to Damascus, a bright light from the sky flashed all around him. Saul fell to the ground, and he heard a voice saying to him, "Saul, Saul, why are you persecuting me?" Saul said, "Who are you, sir?" The reply came, "I am Jesus, whom you are persecuting. Now get up and go into the city and you will be told what you must do." The men who were traveling with Saul heard the voice, but they could see no one. Saul got up from the ground. When he opened his eyes, he couldn't see anything, so the men took Saul's hands and guided him to Damascus. For three days, Saul didn't eat or drink anything, and he couldn't see.

Jesus appeared in a vision to one of His disciples, Ananias. Jesus asked Ananias to go to Saul, for Jesus had chosen Saul to teach the Gentiles—people who are not Jews—about Him. Ananias went to Saul and placed his hands on him, saying, "Saul, my brother, the Lord has sent me, Jesus who appeared to you on the way by which you came, that you may regain your sight and be filled with the holy Spirit." Saul immediately regained his sight, and he was baptized. Saul, also known as Paul, was filled with the Holy Spirit, and he went out and began to teach the people about God. Paul received the gift of grace from the Holy Spirit. With the help of God's grace, Paul was able to know the truth about God and to share the truth about God with others. With the help of God's grace, Paul taught the people about God, proclaiming that Jesus is God the Son.

—based on Acts 9:1–22, 13:9

Like Paul, we need the help of God's grace. We receive grace in the sacraments. Grace takes away original sin. With the help of God's grace, we can overcome some of the effects of original sin. Grace helps us to say "yes" to God. With the help of God's grace, our minds are able to know the truth about God. With the help of God's grace, we are able to make loving choices with our wills. Grace helps us to use self-discipline in what we say and do. With the help of God's grace, we are able to act as images of God. Grace makes it possible for us to live forever with God in heaven.

Complete the following sentences with the correct answer.

1. We receive grace in the _Sacraments_

2. We can overcome some of the effects of _original sin_ with the help of God's grace.

3. _Grace_ takes away original sin.

4. Grace helps us to use _self discipline_ in what we say and do.

5. Grace helps us to say _"yes"_ to God.

6. With the help of God's grace we are able to make _loving choices_ with our wills.

7. Grace makes it possible for us to live forever with God in _Heaven_.

8. With the help of God's grace, our minds are able to know the _truth_ about God.

9. With the help of God's grace, we are able to act as _images_ of God.

The Theological Virtues

If we are to love as God loves, we must share God's life. Grace is God's life in us. Grace enlightens our minds, strengthens our wills, and helps us use self-discipline in the things we say and do. Grace helps us act as images of God. Grace makes it possible for us to live forever with God in heaven.

When we received grace in Baptism, we also received the theological virtues.

The **theological virtues** are supernatural powers that help us to believe in God (faith), to trust in Him (hope), and to love Him (charity). By believing in God, trusting in God, and loving God, we can get to heaven.

In your own words, tell what each theological virtue is.

Faith _Faith in God, Believe in God._

Hope _Hope we get to heaven._

Charity _Giving our time and talents to others_

The Moral Virtues

When we received grace in Baptism, we also received the moral virtues. The **moral virtues** are the supernatural powers that help us to lead moral, or good, lives. They help us to treat persons and things in the right way—the way images of God should.

The principal moral virtues are prudence, justice, fortitude, and temperance.

Prudence helps us make a right choice in a specific situation.
Justice helps us to give people what belongs to them.
Fortitude helps us do the right thing, even when it is difficult.
Temperance helps us control our desires and to use correctly the things that please our senses.

For each moral virtue, give an example of someone exercising that virtue:

Prudence *helps us make the right choice*

Justice *helps you to give back what isn't yours*

Fortitude *helps us do the right thing*

Temperance *helps us control your actions*

A STORY OF FAITH

There have always been men and women who have followed Jesus and tried to act as images of God. With the help of God's grace, and with the theological and moral virtues, they have been able to believe in God, to trust Him, and to love Him. They have been able to lead good and moral lives. One of these people was a woman named Clare. With the help of God's grace, Clare devoted her entire life to loving and serving God and others.

Saint Clare of Assisi

CLARE was born in Assisi, Italy, in the year 1193. Clare's family were members of the nobility. They held a high rank or title, and Clare was known as Lady Clare. Clare obeyed her parents, and she was loving to others. She also cared for the poor.

After Clare's father died, her mother was in charge of Clare and her two sisters. One of Clare's uncles helped to guide the family.

When Clare was eighteen, her mother and uncles tried to interest her in some young men. They hoped that Clare would marry a rich and noble knight. At that time, marriages were often arranged based on the qualities of the girl and the wealth of the boy's family. Clare was a very lovely girl, with beautiful long hair. Many men would have liked to marry her. Clare, however, had a mind of her own. She didn't know why, but she didn't want to get married. It was Saint Francis of Assisi who helped Clare understand that God wanted her to become a nun.

Clare was eager to hear about Francis—about what he taught and his way of life. She would often ask her family about Francis, even though she knew that they would become angry at the mention of his name. In fact, many of the rich and noble families became angry at the mention of Francis' name, because many of their sons were following Francis. Francis was from a wealthy family, yet he had given away all his possessions. He lived a life of poverty and devoted his life to God. He preached to the people about God, and many young men of the nobility were drawn to what Francis taught and to his way of life. These young men decided to follow Francis and to devote their lives to God. They gave away all their possessions and fancy clothes and dressed in rough sackcloth to live a life of poverty.

The life Francis had chosen and the things he preached were completely opposite to anything Clare had ever heard. Clare wanted to meet and speak to Francis, so one day she went to a road on which she knew Francis would be traveling. There, she talked to him; and over the next few months Francis and Clare met and talked about God. Francis talked to Clare about devoting her life to God. Clare decided to do exactly that. On Palm Sunday evening, Clare left her home and family, never to return. A friend went with Clare to a chapel where they were to meet Francis and a priest. Clare gave up her beautiful clothes for a rough habit with a piece of rope tied around her waist. Francis cut off her beautiful hair and placed a rough wool cloth over her head. Clare went to live with some Benedictine nuns until a convent could be set up for her.

When Clare's uncles heard that Clare had become a nun, they were very angry. They went to the Benedictine convent. They found Clare in the church, where she stood holding onto the altar cloth. They tried to persuade Clare to leave the convent and return home. At first they used kind words, but then they tried physical force. Clare hung onto the altar cloth and prayed to God, Mary, and the angels and saints, asking them to help her. No matter how hard Clare's uncles and their men tried to move Clare, they were unable to get her loose from the altar. Clare went back inside the convent, and they never saw her again.

A convent was set up for Clare just outside the city of Assisi. Clare moved there, and each day her sister Agnes came to visit. Agnes saw a great change and happiness in Clare. Clare taught Agnes that the only thing that was important was to love Jesus. Agnes, who was fifteen years old, decided to stay with Clare and devote her life to Jesus, too.

When their uncles heard of this, they went to the convent and dragged Agnes away. Agnes called out to Clare for help. Agnes' uncles dragged her through a thick forest, and the branches tore at her clothes and hair. Soon Agnes was covered with cuts and bruises. Agnes was in pain and so exhausted that she collapsed on the ground. The men tried to drag her along the ground, but suddenly her body became so heavy they were unable to move her. When one of her uncles tried to strike her, a great pain paralyzed his arm, and he was unable to hit her. Her uncles became afraid, seeing that they were going against the will of Jesus. They ran off and never returned. Clare herself found Agnes; and as she gently lifted her sister from the ground, all of the cuts and bruises disappeared, and Agnes didn't remember anything that had happened to her.

Many other women from families in Assisi joined Clare, and so did women from all over Italy and Europe. Even Clare's mother joined her. Many of these women were from wealthy families. Like Clare, they had been accustomed to living in luxury. They joined Clare in moving to the Church of San Damiano and setting up a convent there. They all gave up their possessions and an easy life and lived in absolute poverty. They wore rough habits and wore neither socks nor sandals even when it was very cold. They had no beds; instead, they slept on twigs. Wind and rain came in through cracks in the convent's ceiling. They begged for what little food they ate. They never ate meat. Clare fasted a great deal. Once, Clare was fasting so much that Francis had to order her to eat something each day.

Clare and these women formed a religious order called the Poor Clares. Clare became the abbess (or head) of the order. She was wise and loving and set a good example for all the women in the order. She was responsible for their spiritual and physical well-being. She was like a mother to them all and loved, cared for, and served them.

Jesus allowed Francis to receive the stigmata. Francis had wounds in his hands, his feet, and his side—in imitation of the wounds Jesus received when He was crucified. The wounds Francis received were very painful. He suffered with them for two years. During this time, Francis became almost blind, and his body was in great pain from the stigmata and from his hard life.

Word came to the convent that Francis was dying. Clare wanted to see Francis before he died, but because of her own hard life of strict poverty and fasting, she was too ill to leave the convent. Unable to see Francis again before he died, she was filled with deep sorrow and wept. Francis' body was brought to the church of San Damiano. With the help of her sisters, Clare was taken to the church. She kissed Francis' wounds, looked at him one last time, and then was returned to the convent.

Clare lived another 27 years after the death of Francis. During this time, a German prince named Frederick II decided he wanted an empire that would include Assisi and other lands. He got a group of Arab soldiers together and paid them to be his army. The Convent of San Damiano stood between the army and the city of Assisi. The Arab soldiers hated Christians and decided to attack the convent. Clare was sick in bed, and the frightened nuns went to Clare and asked what they should do. Two nuns helped Clare out of bed. Clare went to their convent chapel and removed a monstrance containing the Holy Eucharist. She went to a large open window and prayed,

A monstrance.

asking Jesus to protect them and the city of Assisi. The Lord answered her. He told her that He would always protect her, and that the city of Assisi was under His protection, too. Clare told her nuns that they would be safe and to have faith in Jesus. Clare then held the monstrance high in the air. The Arab soldiers stopped when they saw Clare at the window, holding the monstrance in her hand. They were filled with fear and ran from the convent. The soldiers didn't attack the city of Assisi either. This event is known as the miracle of the Eucharist of Assisi.

Another miracle occurred when Pope Gregory IX went to Assisi for the canonization of Saint Francis. The Pope and the cardinals with him stopped at the convent of San Damiano. Clare and her nuns were very happy to have the Pope visit and wanted to hear what he had to say. The Pope, however, knew he was in the presence of a saint and wanted to hear Clare speak. Clare invited the Pope and the cardinals for lunch, which consisted of stale bread. The Pope accepted the invitation. When Clare asked the Pope to bless the meal, he asked her to bless it, but out of humility Clare said she couldn't. So the Pope ordered Clare to bless the food. Clare obeyed and blessed the bread with great love and respect. When she finished, everyone looked at the bread in amazement. On each piece of bread, a large cross was formed.

On Christmas Eve, one year before she died, Clare was sick in bed. She wanted to go to Midnight Mass with her nuns but was too ill. As she lay in her bed, a great light filled the room. Suddenly she saw the Midnight Mass. Then, she saw Bethlehem as it was twelve hundred years before. She saw the cave where Jesus was born. Mary and Joseph were there. Jesus appeared to Clare as a grown man and gave Holy Communion to her. (Because of this experience, Clare has been declared the patron saint of television.)

Clare died on August 11, 1253. Two years later she was declared a saint. Like Clare, with the help of God's grace, we can love God and act as His images.

14

We Receive Grace in the Sacraments

What is a sacrament?
A physical sign, given to us by Jesus, through which Jesus meets us and gives us grace.

What are the seven sacraments?
Baptism, Confirmation, Holy Eucharist, Reconciliation, Matrimony, Holy Orders, and Anointing of the Sick.

How does the grace we receive in Baptism help us?
Original sin is taken away; we are able to love God and others here on earth and someday in heaven; we become members of God's family, the Church.

How does the grace we receive in Confirmation help us?
The grace in Confirmation makes it possible for us to love God and others in a mature way. The grace in Confirmation helps us to be witnesses to Jesus.

How does the grace we receive in the Holy Eucharist help us?
The grace in the Holy Eucharist helps us to continue to love God and to love others in a kind and merciful way, the way that Jesus loves us.

How does the grace we receive in the sacrament of Reconciliation help us?
Our sins are forgiven and we are drawn closer to God. The grace we receive makes it possible for us to return God's love. It also makes it possible for us to love and to forgive others the way Jesus loves and forgives us.

How does the grace we receive in the sacrament of Matrimony help us?
The grace of Matrimony makes it possible for the bride and groom to love each other the way Jesus loves us. They can help each other and their children grow in the love of God. They can help each other get to heaven.

Continues

How does the grace we receive in the sacrament of Holy Orders help us?

The grace in Holy Orders enables those men who receive the sacrament to teach the gospel, to celebrate the sacraments, and to do works of love and charity.

How does the grace we receive in the sacrament of the Anointing of the Sick help us?

It heals people from sin and gives them strength to offer their pain and suffering to God in the way Jesus offered His pain and suffering to God. People who receive this sacrament are comforted by Jesus, and sometimes are physically healed.

Jesus asks us not to move away from Him who is "the true vine"— that is, not to lose "grace"—in order not to become dry and useless branches. . . .

Therefore I too urge you, like Jesus: keep innocence! Live in God's grace. Do not let yourselves be attracted, enveloped, swept along and suffocated by evil, which—as you know—always exists in the world and also in ourselves, in view of our nature, which is, certainly, redeemed, but wounded by original sin.

POPE JOHN PAUL II

Vocabulary

sacrament: a physical sign, given to us by Jesus, through which Jesus meets us and gives us grace.

ordination: the consecration of a sacred minister—deacon, priest, or bishop—through the sacrament of Holy Orders.

The Seven Sacraments

Jesus loved and touched people two thousand years ago. Now Jesus loves us and touches us through the sacraments. Jesus gave the Church seven sacraments through which we can experience His gentle and loving touch. The sacraments show us the love Jesus has for us. We receive the love of Jesus through the sacraments. The sacraments are physical signs that Jesus gave us so that we can meet Jesus and receive His grace. Jesus gives us grace so that we are able to love God and others here on earth and some-day in heaven.

The seven sacraments are: Baptism, Confirmation, Holy Eucharist, Reconciliation, Matrimony, Holy Orders, and the Anointing of the Sick. Each sacrament has a different sign. In each sacrament, the sign shows us how Jesus loves us in a merciful way. When Jesus loves us through the sacraments, He gives us grace. The grace we receive helps us to love God and others.

We receive the sacraments through the Church. The deacons, priests, and bishops act for Jesus. When a deacon, priest, or bishop celebrates a sacrament, it is really Jesus Who is celebrating the sacrament.

For it is faith in God which makes the real difference in your lives. Be faithful to your daily prayers. They will keep your faith alive and active.

Only then will you be able to experience the great power of the Lord and also to measure how grown-up your Baptismal faith has become.
—Pope John Paul II

Sacrament of Baptism

The first sacrament we receive is the sacrament of Baptism. Usually, a person is baptized as a baby. The sign of Baptism is the water and the words said by the person baptizing, usually a priest or deacon. Water is poured over the forehead of the person to be baptized while the priest (or deacon) says the words, "I baptize you in the name of the Father, and of the Son, and of the Holy Spirit."

In the sacrament of Baptism, Jesus loves us in a special way. His loving touch takes away original sin. When an adult is baptized, Jesus' loving touch takes away original sin and any sins the person may have committed. Jesus repairs the damage sin has done to our relationship with God. The grace we receive makes it possible for us to love God and others here on earth and someday in heaven. When we are baptized, we become members of God's family, the Church.

Usually we are not old enough to talk when we are baptized, so our parents and godparents speak for us. They say that they believe in God, our loving Father; in His Son, Jesus Christ, our Savior; and in the Holy Spirit. Our parents and godparents promise that they will help us stay away from evil. They promise that they will help us live as images of God.

Along with the grace we receive at Baptism, we receive the theological virtues of faith, hope, and charity, as well as the moral virtues of prudence, justice, fortitude, and temperance. The theological virtues help us know, trust, and love God. The moral virtues help us live good lives.

Sacrament of Confirmation

The sacrament of Confirmation is usually received when a person is a teenager. Remember, we usually receive Baptism as a baby. The grace we receive in Baptism helps us to love God and others. When we are older, we need to love God and others in a more grown-up way than when we were children.

> Remember that the laying on of hands and the sign of the cross with holy chrism will make you more perfectly like Christ and give you the grace and the obligation to spread His "fragrance" among men (2 Corinthians 2:15).
> —Pope John Paul II

The sacrament of Confirmation is usually celebrated by a bishop. The sign of Confirmation is the oil (chrism) and the words said by the bishop. The bishop lays his hands upon the head of the person receiving the sacrament. Then the bishop traces the shape of a cross on the person's forehead with chrism as he says the name of the person, followed by the words "Be sealed with the Gift of the Holy Spirit."

When the bishop does these things and says these words, Jesus touches the person receiving the sacrament and gives the Holy Spirit to the person. In Confirmation, Jesus loves us in a merciful way, and we are able to return God's love. Because we receive the Holy Spirit, we are drawn closer to God. The grace we receive in the sacrament of Confirmation makes it possible for us to love God and others in a mature way. It also helps us to be faithful witnesses to Christ.

Sacrament of the Holy Eucharist

We usually receive the sacrament of the Holy Eucharist for the first time when we are about eight years old and make our First Holy Communion. After our First Communion, we may receive this sacrament often. In the sacrament of the Holy Eucharist, the sign is the bread and wine and the words of consecration (the words spoken by the priest over the bread and wine). At the Consecration of the Mass, the priest says the words of Jesus, "This is my body", over the bread and, "This is the cup of my blood", over the wine. The bread becomes the Body of Jesus, and the wine becomes the Blood of Jesus. At every Mass, Jesus' sacrifice on the Cross is re-presented. Jesus, present in the Eucharist, remains in the tabernacles of our churches so that we can visit Him and pray to Him. The Holy Eucharist is the greatest of the sacraments.

> *Jesus is present with us. . . . Jesus is present in the Eucharist to be met, loved, received, and consoled. . . . Jesus is your greatest Friend. In all the situations of your life, turn to the Divine Friend, present in us with His "grace", present with us and in us in the Eucharist. . . . In fact, in the Eucharist it is Jesus Himself who is waiting for us and whom we will meet one day openly in heaven.*
> —Pope John Paul II

We know that the grace we receive in the other sacraments makes it possible for us to love God and others. Sometimes it is hard to love and to act as images of God, so we need Jesus' help. In the sacrament of the Holy Eucharist, Jesus touches us and gives us this help. Jesus gives Himself to us in Holy Communion. When we receive the Body and Blood of Jesus in Holy Communion, He renews His life (grace) in us. The grace we receive in the sacrament of the Holy Eucharist helps us to continue to love God and to love others in a kind and merciful way, the way that Jesus loves us.

Sacrament of Reconciliation

Even with God's grace, we sometimes make wrong choices, and we do not love God and others the way Jesus does. In other words, we sin. Sin weakens the love between God and us. In order to strengthen our friendship with God and others, we should admit our sins. We should be sorry for our sins, and we should tell God that we are sorry. We can do this in the sacrament of Reconciliation. We may, and should, receive this sacrament often.

The sign of the sacrament of Reconciliation is the sorrow we have when we say our sins to the priest and the words of forgiveness said by the priest. In this sacrament, Jesus touches us, forgiving our sins and drawing us closer to God. The grace that Jesus gives us makes it possible for us to return God's love and makes it possible for us to love and to forgive others the way Jesus loves and forgives us.

> *We know that by sin the Lord is offended, friendship with Him is broken, His grace is lost, one strays from the right path, heading for ruin*
> —Pope John Paul II

Sacrament of Matrimony

In the sacrament of Matrimony (marriage) a man and a woman make a promise to love and to care for each other for the rest of their lives. The sign of the sacrament of Matrimony is the bride and the groom and the "yes" of the vows (promises) they make to one another. The bride and groom make these sacred vows before witnesses: before God, the deacon or priest, and at least two other people. The bride and groom promise before God to love and to care for each other for the rest of their lives—in good times and in bad times, in sickness and in health. These sacred vows are very special. The bride and groom must try hard not to break these promises or vows.

> *In Jesus, Mary, and Joseph there is a real example of unity and communion with all other families. Every other family must look to that divine model and live together with it in order to solve the problems of life.*
> —Pope John Paul II

When two people marry, they become a family. Usually their family grows to include children. The grace that Jesus gives in the sacrament of Matrimony, when He touches the bride and groom, makes it possible for them to love each other the way Jesus loves us. They can help each other and their children get to heaven.

Christ calls many from among you to this extraordinary adventure. He wants to speak to people of today through your voice. He wants to consecrate the Eucharist and forgive sins through you. He wants to live with your hearts. He wants to help with your hands. He wants to save through your efforts.
—Pope John Paul II

Sacrament of Holy Orders

When Jesus lived on earth, He loved the people, taught them, and forgave their sins. At the Last Supper, Jesus celebrated the Holy Eucharist. Jesus asked the Apostles to carry on His work in a special way. Before the Apostles died, they ordained other men to carry on the work of Jesus in a specific way, through the sacrament of Holy Orders. Today, God calls some people to serve Him and to carry on the work of Jesus as deacons, priests, or bishops. These men study and work hard. After a man is prepared and approved by the Church, he is ordained. He is touched by Jesus in the sacrament of Holy Orders. The sacrament of Holy Orders is celebrated by a bishop. There is a special Mass. The man who is to be ordained tells the community he wants to become a deacon, a priest, or a bishop. He promises to be a good leader. The bishop lays his hands upon the head of the man receiving the sacrament. The bishop says a special prayer for the man. The sign of the sacrament of Holy Orders is the bishop laying his hands upon the head of the man receiving the sacrament and the prayer the bishop says for the man. In the sacrament of Holy Orders the bishop ordains men to carry on the work of Jesus in a specific way.

A man ordained as a deacon receives graces that enable him to celebrate some sacraments (Baptism and Matrimony) and help him to do works of charity. Through his works of charity, the deacon helps us to know how to love God and others.

A man ordained as a priest has already received the sacrament of Holy Orders, when he became a deacon. When he is ordained as a priest, he receives graces that make him able to celebrate all of the sacraments except the sacrament of Holy Orders.

Sometimes a priest will be ordained a bishop. Through his ordination as a bishop, he is able to celebrate all of the sacraments and to teach as the Apostles taught.

Sacrament of the Anointing of the Sick

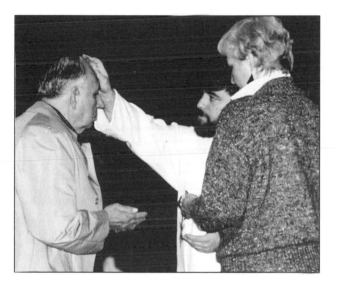

Jesus loves all people. Through His healing touch, Jesus cured many people when He was on earth. People who are sick or suffering need Jesus even more. Today we are still able to experience Jesus' healing touch. When people are very ill, or when elderly people are not in good health, they may receive the sacrament of the Anointing of the Sick. In this sacrament the priest, who acts for Jesus, says a prayer and anoints the person with the oil of the sick on the forehead and on the palms of the hands. The sign of the Sacrament of Anointing of the Sick is the prayer the priest says and the oil of the sick. In the sacrament of the Anointing of the Sick, Jesus comforts and loves the person receiving the sacrament. Jesus touches the person, forgives the person's sins, and draws the person close to God. Sometimes, Jesus restores sick people to health through the sacrament of the Anointing of the Sick.

The grace a person receives from this sacrament heals the person from sin and helps that person to love God and others in a merciful way. The grace strengthens sick or elderly persons and makes them able to offer their pain and suffering to God in the way Jesus offered His pain and suffering to God. They are able to experience God's love.

Life, long or short, is a journey towards paradise: there is our fatherland, there is our real home; there is our appointment! Jesus is waiting for us in paradise!
—Pope John Paul II

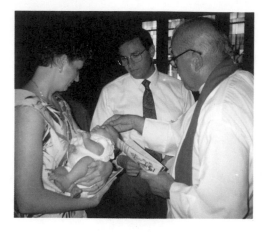 

Fill in the blanks with the name of the appropriate sacrament.

1   The grace that is received strengthens and helps the person to offer any pain and suffering to God.

   _____

2   The sign of this sacrament is bread and wine and the words the priest speaks over the bread and wine.

   _____

3   The grace of this sacrament makes it possible for a husband and a wife to love each other the way Jesus loves us.

   _____

4   The person receiving this sacrament receives graces that enable him to celebrate some sacraments and to do works of love and charity.

   _____

5   The grace we receive makes it possible for us to love God and others in a mature way.

   _____

6   Jesus loves us in a special way that takes away original sin.

   _____

7   By forgiving our sins, Jesus shows us that we should forgive others.

   _____

There are many saints who knew how important the sacraments are. Here are stories about Saint Tarcisius and Saint John Vianney. Think about the importance of the sacraments in their lives.

Saint Tarcisius

AROUND A.D. 258, the Roman Empire was ruled by people who did not like Christians. Christians were not allowed to attend church. The Christians wanted to be able to receive the Eucharist and to pray together. They would meet in underground chambers, called catacombs. Pope Sixtus II himself joined the Christians meeting in the catacombs.

The government ordered its soldiers to arrest as many Christians as they could. Many Christians were put into prison.

Even though they were in prison, the Christians sang songs in praise of God. Tarcisius was a young Christian boy who often walked by the prison. He would stop and listen to the prisoners singing.

One day Tarcisius' father had to go into hiding to avoid being arrested. Tarcisius was very sad. His mother had already been killed because she believed in Jesus. That same evening, Tarcisius went to the catacombs. Pope Sixtus was already there, along with many other Christians. The Pope told them that many of the Christians in prison would be put to death the next day.

One of the Christians with those in the catacombs was a young soldier. He said, "I saw the prisoners today. They want to receive the Holy Eucharist before they die." Even though it was dangerous to try to get the Holy Eucharist into the prison, many people volunteered to do it! Tarcisius begged to be chosen, but everyone thought he was too young. Tarcisius argued that because he was young, no one would pay any attention to him. This argument persuaded the Pope. Tarcisius promised to carry the Holy Eucharist close to his heart and to be very careful.

The next day Tarcisius hid the Holy Eucharist under his shirt, close to his heart. He crossed his arms over his chest for extra protection. He began to walk to the prison.

Along the way, Tarcisius saw a group of boys playing in the street. Tarcisius sometimes played with them. They were getting ready to have another stone-throwing contest—to see who could throw a stone the farthest. They saw Tarcisius and called to him. Tarcisius had won an earlier stone-throwing contest, so they wanted him to join them. "Come on, play with us!" they said.

Tarcisius answered, "No, I have something I must do."

"Forget it! Join our game!" All of the boys already held stones in their hands.

"I can't", replied Tarcisius. The boys formed a circle around him. One of them asked, "What are you hiding? Why are you crossing your arms like that?"

Tarcisius wouldn't answer. He tried to continue on his mission, but the boys wouldn't let him through the circle. They made the circle smaller.

Tarcisius begged them to let him go. He still would not tell them that he was holding the Holy Eucharist.

Finally, he was able to break out of the circle. Someone yelled, "Let's get him with the stones!" The boys began to throw stones at him. The stones hit him from all directions. He finally collapsed, but he was still able to hold the Eucharist tightly.

Tarcisius was weak and dying. Tarcisius whispered, "Dear Jesus, I've protected You. I love You." Then, with the Holy Eucharist still held tightly to his heart, Tarcisius died. When his attackers searched him, miraculously the Host had disappeared.

Some Christians found the body of Tarcisius and carried it to Pope Sixtus. Pope Sixtus looked at Tarcisius' lifeless body and said, "Jesus is safe, Tarcisius, because of your great love."

Tarcisius died rather than let anything happen to the Holy Eucharist. Tarcisius is the patron saint of children making their first Holy Communion. He is also one of the patron saints of altar boys.

Saint John Vianney

JOHN VIANNEY was born in Dardilly, France, on May 8, 1786, and was baptized on the same day. John's father was a farmer. John's mother took care of the home and cared for John and his sisters and brothers. John's father told the children about the stars in the sky and the best time to plant seeds. His mother told them Bible stories. It was the Bible stories that John remembered and liked the most.

When John was old enough, he helped on the farm by weeding the garden, feeding the chickens, and gathering eggs. When John was seven, he was old enough to become a shepherd. He took the sheep to the pasture each day and watched over them.

During these years, it was difficult for the Vianney family to go to Mass. The French Revolution had begun in 1789, and the government persecuted those Catholics who followed the Pope. Churches and monasteries were closed. Priests and nuns who followed the Pope and acknowledged him as head of the Church on earth were killed. Some of the loyal priests dressed as farmers or peddlers. They would celebrate Mass and hear confessions in selected barns or farm houses. This was done in secret. So, late at night, John Vianney, his family, and other good families would go to the selected meeting place for confession and Mass.

John was very interested in the priests who risked their lives in order to celebrate Mass and the sacraments. John's mother explained to him that the men who were priests had been called by God. They were called to do this special work and to act for Jesus on earth. Through the priests, Jesus takes away original sin in Baptism and forgives sins in Reconciliation. Jesus gives Himself, His Body and Blood, to us in the Holy Eucharist and sends the Holy Spirit to help us in Confirmation. Jesus brings men and women together in Matrimony. He forgives, loves, and comforts those who are sick or dying in the sacrament of Anointing of the Sick. Then, through Holy Orders celebrated by a bishop, Jesus gives the power of the priesthood to other men. In the sacraments, the deacon, priest, or bishop acts for Jesus.

John thought it would be wonderful to be called to be a priest. He even pretended to be a priest. When he was out in the pasture with his younger sister and the other shepherd children, he would pretend that he was their priest and that they were his congregation. Together they would pray the Rosary and sing songs praising God. They even marched in procession behind a cross they had made. Then John would give a short sermon to his little congregation.

When John was older, he spent some time visiting his aunt in another town. There he had a small amount of schooling, and he also studied for his First Holy Communion. He had received the sacrament of Reconciliation two years earlier. The First Communion classes were held in secret. If the teachers and students had been caught studying religion, they would have been in a lot of trouble.

John was very, very happy when he received the sacrament of the Holy Eucharist for the first time. This also had to be done in secret. After his First Holy Communion, John returned home to work on the farm. He helped plow the fields, gather wood, take care of the cattle, and do other chores. Each morning, John prayed, asking Mary to help him in his work.

In 1802, when John was sixteen years old, the persecution ended. Catholics could again openly study and profess their faith without fearing for their lives. Priests and nuns resumed their work openly in the churches and monasteries.

John wanted to become a priest, but he didn't know if he would be accepted. He could read and write very little, and he wasn't sure if he could learn Latin, theology, and all the other subjects he would need to study to be a priest.

John talked to his father, but his father wouldn't allow him to study for the priesthood. He wanted to keep John at home to help with work on the farm. John and his mother prayed that John's father would change his mind, and a few years later he did.

A priest named Father Balley ran a seminary school for young men interested in becoming priests. John was not accepted as a seminarian right away, because Father Balley didn't think John had a vocation. Finally, after talking with John, Father Balley agreed to accept him. John was very happy, and preparations were made for him to begin his studies for the priesthood.

But another problem arose for John. He'd had only a small amount of schooling, and soon he found that the classes were very hard for him. Latin was the most difficult for him, so another student helped him study. John prayed for help with his studies. He received the sacrament of Confirmation. Gradually, John had more success in his studies.

However, yet another problem presented itself. John received a notice that he had to join the army. John was very sad, but he went to report for duty. Soon after, he became very sick and had to be taken to the hospital. When he was released from the hospital, he tried to rejoin the military group he was assigned to, but because he was not fully recovered from his illness, he wasn't able to reach them. As a result, he was considered a deserter and had to go into hiding. A kind family gave John shelter in their barn, and he helped with the work around the farm. Finally, he received a pardon and was able to return to his studies under Father Balley.

Shortly after John returned, his mother died, and he was filled with sorrow. She had encouraged him in his desire to become a priest. He prayed, asking his mother to pray for him. He continued his studies at the seminary, but he couldn't keep up with the work. The lectures were given in Latin, and John still couldn't understand Latin very well. So, after nine years of study, John was dismissed from the seminary.

John went to see Father Balley to tell him that he had been dismissed from the seminary and that he was thinking of becoming a brother. But Father Balley now thought that John truly had a vocation to the priesthood, and he decided to teach John himself.

With the help of Father Balley, John learned the things he needed to know. He was ordained a deacon. After continuing his studies with Father Balley, he was at last ordained a priest, on August 12, 1815. The bishop placed a stole (a symbol of the priesthood) on John. John asked God to help him become a holy priest and to help the people whom he served get to heaven. Father John Vianney's first assignment was to be an assistant to Father Balley—an assignment that made both priests very happy.

Father Balley died two years later, and Father Vianney was made pastor in a small village called Ars. There was not much love of God in Ars, and Father Vianney's bishop told John to help the people there to love God.

When Father Vianney reached Ars, he found the church in sad disrepair. The roof was damaged, and the interior was covered with dust and cobwebs. Only about twenty people attended Mass on Sundays. The children were not cared for properly, there was no school for them to attend, and there were no religion classes for them. The people couldn't read or write. They went to taverns, where they gambled and got drunk. They used bad language and cursed and swore. The young men and women were most interested in the village dances, which lasted far into the night and sometimes led them into sin. The farms and livestock were neglected, also.

There was so much work to be done that Father Vianney wasn't sure where to begin. He wanted to do so many things. He wanted to teach the people to love God and to put God first in their lives. He wanted them to go to Mass on Sundays—not work in their fields, gamble, or get drunk in the taverns. He wanted the children to be taught about God and to learn about their Faith. He wanted the bad language to stop. He wanted people to act as images of God. The church needed to be repaired. He wanted to build a school so that the children could be taught to read and write.

Father Vianney decided to begin his work by starting religion classes for the children. The classes met every day. He tried to teach the children to love God and to lead holy lives. The religion classes were very successful. Soon some of the adults started going to church in the evening for prayer.

There were still many people who stayed away. Father Vianney was already doing penances for the people of this parish. He fasted every day— eating only one meal of boiled potatoes and a glass of milk. He decided to do extra penances by sleeping only a few hours a night. He used the hours of sleep he gave up to pray. Slowly, he began to see some changes in the people of his parish.

After Father Vianney had been at Ars for about five years, he decided to open a school for girls. There, the girls could learn about God and their Faith. They would learn sewing, cooking, and spinning too, so that they would be able to earn a living. With his own money, Father Vianney bought a building and had it converted into a school. The school was named Providence, and it had 16 girls in its first class, some coming from other towns. The school was free, and over the next four years the number of students rose to 30. In addition to their studies, the children were encouraged to pray

and to offer sacrifices for the people of Ars. They prayed that all the people of Ars would learn to love God. Gradually, more and more people began attending evening prayers and Sunday Mass. All children attended religion classes. There was less drinking, gambling, and unnecessary work on Sundays, and bad language was less often heard. Father Vianney encouraged all the people to have a devotion to the Blessed Virgin Mary. He tried to help the people love her, and he asked the people to pray the "Hail Mary" often and well.

God graced Father Vianney in a special way. This priest of Ars was able to help people know their sins and help them to make good confessions. Many people came to Ars from other villages just so Father Vianney could hear their confessions. They would wait in line, sometimes all night, so that Father Vianney could hear their confessions the following day. Father Vianney also had the grace and ability to pick, out of a long line of people, the persons who needed God's forgiveness the most. Father Vianney heard between one and two hundred confessions a day. He sometimes heard confessions for up to 16 hours each day.

Father Vianney took time for himself only to celebrate Mass; eat his lunch of boiled potatoes; and say his evening prayers. As time went by, his hard work and fasting began to affect his health. He became very sick with pneumonia. His doctor thought Father Vianney would surely die. The people prayed for the recovery of their beloved pastor. Father Vianney asked the Blessed Virgin Mary and Saint Philomena to pray for him, also.

Father Vianney recovered from the pneumonia and went to visit his brother in Dardilly. He was still very weak, and he needed rest. With all his work as a parish priest, he had had little time for prayer. He thought he would have more time to give to prayer if he were a hermit or if he lived in a monastery. The Holy Spirit, however, helped Father Vianney to recognize that his mission was to help people to love God, to turn away from sin, and to live holy lives. While Father Vianney was at his brother's home in Dardilly, the people who usually went to Ars to see him followed him to Dardilly and asked him to hear their confessions. Father Vianney agreed, even though he was not yet fully recovered.

Father Vianney eventually returned to Ars. The people were very happy and went out to meet him as he neared the village. Back at Ars, Father Vianney resumed his work.

The number of people coming to Ars to see Father Vianney increased each month. During the year 1858–59, thousands of people came to Ars to see Father Vianney for confession and for guidance. Even other priests came to ask his advice regarding their work.

In the summer of 1859, Father Vianney became more and more weak. By the end of July, he knew he was dying. The people prayed for Father Vianney's recovery, and he blessed them from his bed. Father Vianney prepared himself for his death by receiving the sacraments of Reconciliation, Holy Eucharist, and Anointing of the Sick. He was filled with peace and joy.

On August 4th, at 2 o'clock in the morning, the bishop and several priests and the friends of Father Vianney were gathered in his room, praying. As Father Vianney listened to the prayers, he thought about how good it was to be dying as a priest. Father John Vianney had spent his life as a parish priest. There had been many responsibilities placed on him, and he had made many sacrifices. He had been a devoted pastor. He had celebrated Mass and the sacraments for his parishioners and many others besides. He had met thousands of people and advised them. He had forgiven their sins and helped them to love God. He had done each day's priestly work as well as he could. He knew that the reward for helping others to know and love God was great. Jesus waited for Father Vianney in paradise.

In that hour Father Vianney died, at age seventy-three. He had been called home by God. John Vianney was declared a saint by Pope Pius XI in 1925. He is the patron saint of parish priests. His feast day is August 4.

Unit 5

Acting As an
Image of God

15

The
Ten Commandments

When we sin are we still images of God?
Yes, but we are not the best images of God at that time.

What did God give us that tells us how to act as images of God?
God gave us the Ten Commandments. They tell us how to be the best images of God we can be.

How does grace help us?
Grace helps us believe what God tells us, helps us act as images of God, and makes it possible for us to live forever with God in heaven.

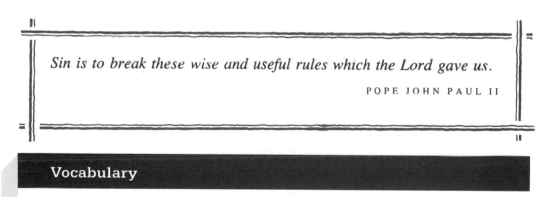

Sin is to break these wise and useful rules which the Lord gave us.

POPE JOHN PAUL II

Vocabulary

commandments: directions God gives us so that we can act as Christ acted.

We Are Images of God

God made us in His image. We have minds to think and wills to make choices. We choose how to act with our wills. We are created to act as Christ did. We can choose to do what is right and act as images of God, or we can choose to do what is wrong.

God gave us the Ten Commandments, which tell us how to act as images of God. The Ten Commandments are directions God gives us so that we can act as Christ acted. If we follow the Ten Commandments, we will become better images of God.

There are always going to be temptations, which make wrong choices look good. It's not always easy to make a right choice. Our feelings are not always accurate signs of whether a choice is right or wrong. Sometimes we can feel happy, even though our choice was a wrong one. Other times we can feel sad, even though we made a right choice. Again, we see that it's not always easy to make a right choice. The Ten Commandments help us to know the right choices. They are a guide for us, to help us judge right from wrong.

When we knowingly and willingly choose not to follow the Ten Commandments, we sin. We are still images of God, but we are not the best images of God that we can be. We are not acting the way we were created to act. When we sin, we hurt God, ourselves, and others. When we follow the first three of God's commandments, we love God by respecting His name, praising Him, and keeping God's day holy. When we follow the other seven of God's commandments, we show that we love ourselves and others, because we do what is good for us and them.

Even when we trust God, it is not always easy to do what He asks us. God gave us the gift of His life, grace, to help us follow the Ten Commandments. Grace helps us believe what God tells us, and it helps us act as images of God. Grace also makes it possible for us to live someday with God in heaven.

Right choices are not always easy. God gave us the Ten Commandments to tell us what the right choices are. The commandments tell us how to love and how to give ourselves to God and others. The more right choices we make, the better images of God we become.

Here is a story about Saint Augustine. As he was growing up, he sometimes made wrong choices.

Saint Augustine

AUGUSTINE was born in the year 354. He was born in the town of Tagaste, in a Roman province of northern Africa. Augustine was not baptized as a child. For a long time, he was not even sure there was a God. Augustine's father, Patricius, was a pagan. He did not believe in Christ. Augustine's mother, Monica, was a Catholic. She prayed every day that Augustine and his father would believe in God and become Catholics, too.

At that time, not every boy was lucky enough to attend school. Augustine was fortunate; he was able to go to school. However, Augustine did not feel that he was lucky. He did not like school. He was smart, but he did not like to study. Augustine was interested only in sports and games. His parents and teachers had to force him to do his lessons.

Augustine made many wrong choices as he was growing up. He did not always respect his parents or his teachers. Sometimes he would have an argument with them or purposely embarrass them. Sometimes he would even steal from them. He would cheat at games in order to win. But he would not allow anyone else to cheat. If he caught other people cheating, he would start a fight with them.

One time, Augustine and some of his friends went out at night and stole pears in an orchard. Then they threw the pears to some pigs. Augustine didn't want or need the pears. He simply enjoyed stealing them.

When Augustine was seventeen years old, he went to the city of Carthage to study. His friend Alypius went with him. This time Augustine studied very hard in school. He still made some wrong choices, however. When he met a girl and fell in love with her, he did not marry her in the Church. He believed many untrue things about God and made fun of holy people. He used his talents to make other people miserable, and he tried to make himself happy. But he was never really happy.

During this time, Augustine received a letter from his mother. His father, Patricius, had died. Monica said that she would miss her husband, but she was happy, because, before he died, Patricius had become a Catholic. Monica said she was still praying that Augustine would believe in God and become a Catholic.

Augustine continued to search for happiness and the cause of evil. He listened to people talk about God and the Catholic Church. One person Augustine listened to was the bishop, Saint Ambrose. Saint Ambrose's teachings began to make an impression on Augustine.

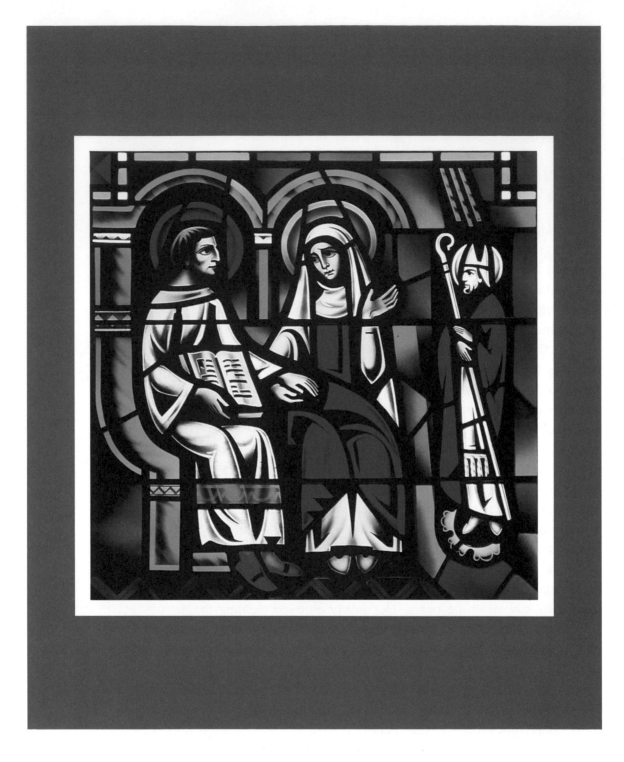

One day, a man named Pontitian came and spoke with Augustine and his friend Alypius. He talked to them about two men who had changed their lives and become devoted to God.

As Pontitian told this story, Augustine reflected on his past sins and was filled with deep sorrow. Augustine left Alypius and went out into the garden. Augustine cried out to God, "And you, O Lord, how long? How long, O Lord, will you be angry forever? Remember not our past iniquities [sins]."

Then he heard, from a nearby house, the voice of a child repeating, over and over, "Take up and read. Take up and read." Understanding this as a direction from God, Augustine got up and hurried back to where Alypius was sitting. There Augustine picked up the book of Saint Paul's epistles and read the first chapter that he saw. He read, "Not in rioting and drunkenness, not in chambering and impurities, not in strife and envying; but put you on the Lord Jesus Christ, . . ." Augustine finally believed and understood, and Augustine's heart was filled with peace.

Augustine told Alypius what had happened to him. A change had taken place in Alypius also. Alypius asked Augustine to show him the passage he had read. Alypius found the next words of the passage, which said, "Now him that is weak in the faith, take unto you." Alypius applied these words to himself.

Together they went and told Augustine's mother, Monica, what had happened. Monica rejoiced and praised God.

On Easter-eve, in 387, Augustine was baptized by Saint Ambrose. Three years later, he was ordained a priest. Eventually, he became the bishop of Hippo. He began to use his talents of writing and speaking to spread the good news of Christ. Augustine is now a saint. His feast day is August 28.

Like Saint Augustine, we sometimes make wrong choices. Right choices are not always easy. The Ten Commandments tell us what the right choices are. With the help of God's grace, we, like Saint Augustine, can change our lives and make right choices.

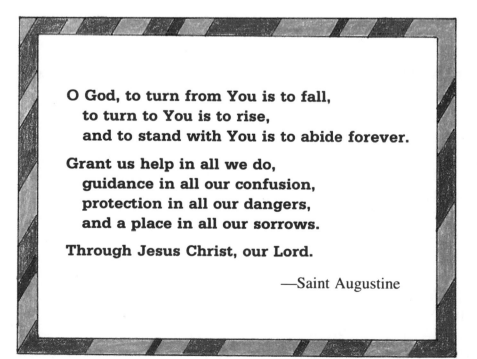

O God, to turn from You is to fall,
  to turn to You is to rise,
  and to stand with You is to abide forever.

Grant us help in all we do,
  guidance in all our confusion,
  protection in all our dangers,
  and a place in all our sorrows.

Through Jesus Christ, our Lord.

—Saint Augustine

Moses

God chose Moses to lead the Israelites out of slavery from Egypt. He led them across the desert to the foot of Mount Sinai, where they set up camp.

One day, God asked Moses to climb to the top of Mount Sinai. Early the next morning, Moses climbed the mountain. Moses spent many days talking to God. God gave Moses two stone tablets with the Ten Commandments written on them.

These are the Ten Commandments:
1. I, the LORD, am your God. You will not have other gods besides me.
2. You will not take the name of the LORD, your God, in vain.
3. Remember to keep holy the sabbath day.
4. Honor your father and your mother.
5. You will not kill.
6. You will not commit adultery.
7. You will not steal.
8. You will not bear false witness against your neighbor.
9. You will not covet your neighbor's wife.
10. You will not covet anything that belongs to your neighbor.
   —based on Exodus 20:1–17

Find the following words in the Word Search. These words were
used in the story of Moses.

OBEY   GOD   LIE

COVET   ADULTERY   HONOR

HOLY   MOSES   STEAL

COMMANDMENTS NEIGHBOR   KILL

SINAI   LORD   LOVE

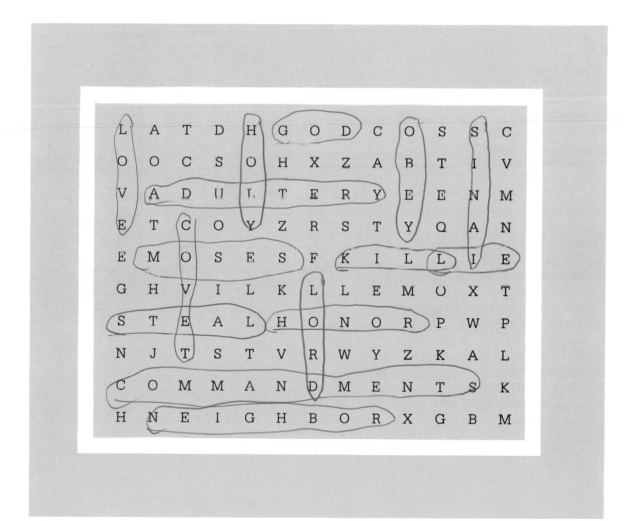

Name: _____

Date: _____

The Ten Commandments

Crossword Puzzle

Across

2. The seventh commandment is: you will not _steal_.
4. You will not _commit_ adultery.
5. _Honor_ your father and your mother.
7. You will not bear false _witness_ against your neighbor.
8. I, the LORD, am your _God_. You will not have other gods besides Me.

Down

1. You will not _____.
2. Remember to keep holy the _____ _____.
3. You will not covet anything that belongs to your _____.
4. You will not _____ your neighbor's wife.
6. You will not take the _____ of the LORD, your God, in vain.

16

Loving God

What are the first three commandments?

1. I, the LORD, am your God. You will not have other gods besides me.
2. You will not take the name of the LORD, your God, in vain.
3. Remember to keep holy the sabbath day.

What do the first three commandments tell us?

The first three commandments tell us how to love God.

What does the first commandment tell us?

There is only one God. We should always put God first in our lives.

What does the second commandment tell us?

We should use God's name with respect and love.

What does the third commandment tell us?

We should make Sundays and Holy Days special. We should attend Mass with God's family and spend time with our families.

Vocabulary

take in vain: to use without respect.

sacrifice: an action whereby someone or something is offered to God as a sign of love.

worship: to praise, love, respect, and honor.

theological virtues: the supernatural powers that help us to believe in God (faith), trust in Him (hope), and love Him (charity).

He alone is the solution to all your problems. He alone is the Way, the Truth, and the Life.

POPE JOHN PAUL II

The First Commandment

I, the LORD, am your God. You will not have other gods besides me.

The commandments are directions God gives us so that we can act as Christ acted. The first commandment asks us to love God above all things. God should be first in our lives. We should be careful not to make material things more important than God. We should be careful not to be greedy. For example, if making money to buy things becomes so important to us that we lose sight of God, we have made money our god.

One way to show our love for God is by worshiping Him. There are several ways we can worship God. We can worship God through prayer. We can pray to God by repeating prayers we have learned or by using our own words. We can pray out loud or silently, with someone or alone.

Our singing or our artwork can also be a form of prayer. Sometimes just thinking about God is a prayer. No matter which way we pray, the important thing is that we are showing God how much we love Him.

We can follow the first commandment by believing in God and trusting Him. We can tell others about Him. We should not be afraid to tell others how important God is to us. We can let others know that, because we are images of God, we should act as God wants us to act.

Another way to follow the first commandment is to perform sacrifices of love for God. When we sacrifice, we give up something that we enjoy to show that God is more important to us than anything or anyone else. The sacrifice might be something small—for example, giving up a television show or our favorite food as an act of love for God. The sacrifice can be something big—for example, the martyrs gave up their lives out of love for God. What makes something a sacrifice is the willingness to give it up because of our love for God. Our sacrifices show that God is more important to us than anything or anyone else.

The Second Commandment

You will not take the name of the LORD, your God, in vain.

God is all loving and good. God created us and loves us. He deserves our praise, respect, love, and honor. We should show our love for God by respecting His name.

The second commandment tells us that we should show our love for God by using His name with respect and love. We should praise God and His name through word and song. When we speak God's name, we should

156   *We Follow Jesus*

do so in a loving and respectful way. We should not use God's name to express anger. We should not use God's name to curse or swear, because God's name is holy.

We should not use God's name in a casual and careless manner. When someone calls you by name, you respond, expecting to have a conversation. Sometimes a person will call your name and then, when you answer, will say, "Never mind." If this happens often, it becomes annoying.

When we say God's name, He is waiting to listen to us. Sometimes people use God's name in conversations without thinking, or out of habit. But even when people say God's name in a casual, careless way, He is still waiting to listen to them. When they do not follow through with a conversation, they are not showing God and His name the love and respect they should.

You have noticed in songs, movies, and books that God's name is sometimes misused. Misuse of God's name shows disrespect for Him and for His name. We are not respectful when we think, say, or do anything that is directed against God, the Church, or the saints. We should not do anything that shows disrespect for God or His name.

The Third Commandment
Remember to keep holy the sabbath day.

The third commandment tells us we should take time to pray and worship God. We do this by attending Mass on Sundays (or Saturday evenings). After we begin the day with God's family at Mass, we spend the rest of the day with our family. If people have to work on Sundays, they still should find time to attend Mass. They should also find time to spend with their familes.

As Catholics we have the responsibility to attend Mass also on Holy Days of obligation.

The first three commandments tell us how to love God. They tell us to place God first in our lives, to respect God's name, and to praise and worship God on Sundays and Holy Days.

The Theological Virtues

To follow the first three commandments, we need to *know* God, to *hope* in Him, and to *love* Him. We can know God, hope in Him, and love Him because in Baptism we received the three theological virtues: faith, hope, and charity (love). As we learned in Lesson 13 ("With the Help of God's Grace"), faith is the supernatural power that God gives us that helps us believe in Him. Hope is the supernatural power that God gives us that helps us to trust Him. And charity (love) is the supernatural power that God gives us that helps us to love Him.

If we do acts of faith, hope, and love, we will be following the first three commandments.

An Act of Faith, Hope, and Love

O my God, I believe that You are one God in three Persons, Father, Son, and Holy Spirit. I believe all the things which You have taught us through Your holy catholic Church. I trust in Your mercy and love. I hope to receive forgiveness for my sins. With the help of Your grace, I hope to live with You in heaven one day. These things are possible because of the suffering, death, and resurrection of Jesus, my Lord and Savior. I love You with all my heart because You deserve all my love. I love others as I should. Amen.

In the following passage from Scripture, omit all the *x*'s and copy the message on the lines below.

Jxexsus rexplxied: "Txhxe fxixrxsxt xis txhxis: 'Hear, x0 Ixsraxxel! Txhe Lxorxd oxuxrx Gxod ixs Lord alxonex! Yxou shxall xlxove the Lxorxd yoxur Gxoxd wxith axll yxouxr hexart, wixtxh alxl yoxur soxul, wxith alxl yoxur mixnxd, axnxd wixth alxl yxoxur stxrexngxth.'"
—Mark 12:29–30

_____

_____

_____

_____

_____

_____

17

Loving Others

What are the fourth through tenth commandments?
4. Honor your father and your mother.
5. You will not kill.
6. You will not commit adultery.
7. You will not steal.
8. You will not bear false witness against your neighbor.
9. You will not covet your neighbor's wife.
10. You will not covet your neighbor's goods.

What do the fourth through tenth commandments tell us?
The fourth through tenth commandments tell us how God loves others and how we, as images of God, should love others.

What does the fourth commandment tell us?
The fourth commandment tells us that we should honor and obey our parents. We should care for our parents when they are older. We should love our parents even after they have died, by praying for them.

What does the fifth commandment tell us?
God loves and cares for all persons He has created. As images of God, we should love, respect, and care for ourselves and others. We should never take the life of another person, including the life of the unborn, the elderly, the physically disabled, and the incurably ill. We should never take our own lives. We should not use harmful drugs. We should care for our bodies properly.

What does the sixth commandment tell us?
The sixth commandment tells us that a man and a woman should not act as a husband and wife if they are not married to each other. We should respect our bodies and the bodies of others. We should be modest in the way we dress and act.

Continues

What does the seventh commandment tell us?

We should not steal—take and keep for ourselves things that belong to others. We should treat the possessions of others with care.

What does the eighth commandment tell us?

We should always tell the truth, we should not spread stories about other people, and we should not cheat.

What does the ninth commandment tell us?

We should not want someone else's husband or wife to be our husband or wife. We should not want someone else's family to be our family.

What does the tenth commandment tell us?

We should not want those things that belong to our neighbors so much that we dislike our neighbors because they have what we want.

God, by means of His commandments, teaches us how we must behave . . . respect for our parents and superiors (fourth commandment), respect for life in all its forms (fifth commandment), respect for the body and love (sixth commandment), respect for what belongs to others (seventh commandment), respect for truth (eighth commandment).

Love life, respect life, in yourselves and in others.

Do not let yourselves be led astray by the tempting atmosphere created by the permissive society which says everything is lawful!

Try to make life beautiful for everyone with obedience, kindness, good manners! The secret of joy is goodness!

You are called to be bearers of generosity and honesty, to fight against immorality, to prepare a more just, healthy, and happy world.

POPE JOHN PAUL II

abortion: taking the life of an unborn child.

euthanasia: taking the life of a person who is suffering from an incurable disease, physical disability, or old age.

suicide: taking one's own life.

adultery: to try to love in a married way someone to whom we are not married.

covet: to want very much what belongs to someone else.

modest: decent; respectful of one's body.

The Fourth Commandment

Honor your father and your mother.

Our parents have the responsibility of teaching us, caring for us, and loving us. Loving parents love us as God loves us, and they want what is best for us. Loving parents choose what is good for us. We may not always see how something our parents ask can be good for us—such as going to bed at a certain time, when we want to stay up and watch TV. But we should obey our parents and follow the rules they have for us.

The fourth commandment has other meanings also. When we are adults we no longer have to do everything our parents ask, but we should always show our parents love and respect.

We should help care for our parents when they are older. We can do this by visiting them and making sure they have the things they need. We can do things for our parents, and we can take them where they need to go if they are not able to get around by themselves. We can show our love for our parents even after they have died, by praying for them.

As children, we should obey our parents and follow the rules they have for us. We should always love and honor our parents.

The Fifth Commandment

You will not kill.

God loves and cares for all persons He has created. As images of God we should love, respect, and care for ourselves and others. God has given each of us the gift of life. Our bodies are a special part of the gift of life we receive from God. Through our bodies—in order words, through our words and actions—we express our persons. Through our bodies we express who we are.

The fifth commandment tells us that we should not harm our bodies or the bodies of other persons. We should never take the life of another person.

Abortion is taking the innocent life of an unborn child. Abortion is a terrible crime because it destroys the life of an innocent person who is helpless and defenseless. A young girl who is not married and finds out that she is going to have a baby may hear that abortion is the answer to her problem. But abortion is never the answer. It would be an unloving act for her to take the life of her unborn child. The loving answer to her situation would be for her to have the child. Then, after having the child, she can choose either to be a parent to her child or to make an adoption plan for her child. We must never take the life of an unborn child. Adoption is a loving act; abortion is a wrong choice.

Sometimes, when a loved one is suffering from an incurable disease, a physical disability, or old age, a relative or friend might be tempted to take the suffering person's life in order to end the suffering. This is called euthanasia, or mercy killing. God loves and cares for all those who suffer from illness, disability, or old age. We should love and care for them as God does. We should do everything we can to help those who are suffering from pain or illness, but we should never directly take a life to end suffering. We should trust that God is caring for those who suffer.

We should never hurt another person's body by hitting. We should never hurt another person's feelings by name-calling.

You should also love and care for yourself. You must never take your own life. Taking your own life means that you do not love yourself as God loves you. A person thinking about committing suicide is in need of help and should talk to a trusted adult right away.

We should take care of our bodies by eating properly, by getting enough sleep and exercise, and by not taking harmful drugs. Drinking too much alcohol and smoking too much can also harm our bodies, so we should not do these things.

The Sixth Commandment
You will not commit adultery.

When a man and a woman get married, they join their lives together and promise to love only each other in a special way for their whole lives. They promise to love and to care for each other, to want what is best for each other, and to help each other grow in love for God and others. A husband and wife share a very special love relationship with each other. It is wrong if they share their special love with another person. This is called adultery. Persons committing adultery hurt themselves and their families. They especially hurt the special relationship they share with their husband or wife.

A man and a woman should not act as husband and wife until they are married. It is wrong when two people who are not married try to act as husband and wife, because they are not loving each other the way God intended.

We are made in the image of God. God is good, and God made us good. This means that our bodies are good. We should respect our bodies and the bodies of others. We should not make fun of any part of our bodies or the bodies of others. We should stay away from literature, movies, songs, and language that encourage disrespect for the human body. We should also be modest in the way we dress and act. The clothes we wear should be appropriate to where we are. We should respect other people's privacy by knocking on bedroom and bathroom doors before we enter.

The Seventh Commandment
You will not steal.

Everyone has the right to own things. We should respect that right and not take and keep for ourselves things that belong to others. We should be careful with, and not abuse, the things God has given us. We should also be careful with, and not abuse, the things that belong to others. We should not scribble in library or school books, because they belong to the library or to the school. Scribbling in the books can ruin someone else's enjoyment of them. We should also be careful with the things we borrow from someone else. We should not write or draw on the walls of buildings or bathrooms. These are examples of property that belongs to others, and we should treat other people's property with respect.

The Eighth Commandment
You will not bear false witness against your neighbor.

This commandment means that we should be honest and truthful. As images of God, we should act as Christ acted. God does not lie. Jesus would not have cheated on tests or changed the rules of a game just so He could win. He did not spread stories that hurt someone's reputation. Telling the truth—being honest—is not always easy, but it is something we must do. When we lie, we are not thinking about God or others; we are being selfish. We are not acting as images of God.

The Ninth Commandment
You will not covet your neighbor's wife.

To covet someone means to want a person to belong to you. When we want someone else's brother or sister or mom or dad, instead of our own, we are coveting them. God gave each of us a special family. We should be happy with the family we have. It would also be wrong to want (or covet) someone else's husband or wife to be yours.

The Tenth Commandment
You will not covet your neighbor's goods.

God has given each of us special things. The things God has given us are not the same things He has given others. We should not be envious of what others have. We should try to be happy with what God has given us.

There are holy men and women who live with God in heaven. They followed Jesus while they were living on earth. They tried to follow the Ten Commandments and act as images of God. These holy people are called saints.

Loving God and others by following Jesus and the Ten Commandments is not always easy. We are able to do so only with God's help. Saint Elizabeth Ann Seton often turned to God in prayer to seek help, guidance, and comfort. Read this story about the first person born in the United States to be declared a saint.

Saint Elizabeth Ann Seton

ELIZABETH BAYLEY was born on August 28, 1774, just before the American Revolutionary War began. Elizabeth's father, Richard Bayley, was a doctor. Although he cared for some wealthy patients in order to earn money to provide for his family, Dr. Bayley spent much of his time caring for the poor.

Elizabeth had two sisters, Mary and Catherine. Mary was older than Elizabeth, and Catherine was younger. Elizabeth was only two years old when her mother died at the time of Catherine's birth.

Richard Bayley remarried, and Elizabeth and her sisters had a stepmother who cared for them. Mrs. Bayley was a very religious woman. She taught the girls their prayers and raised them in her Protestant faith.

Elizabeth remembered the mother she had known as a baby and missed her very much. She thought that her mother was in heaven. So when her little sister, Catherine, died, Elizabeth did not cry, because she thought that Catherine had gone up to heaven and could be with their mother.

Elizabeth's father made sure that she had a good education. Elizabeth went to school, and she loved to read. She often read the Bible. Elizabeth learned how to speak and write French. She learned how to sew, play the piano, and ride a horse. These were things that young ladies of wealthy families were expected to know.

As a schoolgirl, Elizabeth spent some of her time caring for the poor and ill. She was very concerned about them. Even as a teenager she cared for the sick and brought food baskets to the poor.

When Elizabeth was nineteen years old, she married William Seton. They were happy together and loved each other very much. They had five children born to them—three girls and two boys. William and his father ran a shipping business together. William was able to provide very well for his family. They lived in a beautiful and comfortable home in New York.

Their life contrasted greatly with the lives of the people living in the slums of the city. In the slums, the people lived in shacks. The slums were crowded and dirty, and the houses that had no windows smelled horrible. Elizabeth visited, loved, and cared for the poor people living there. It was especially hard for her to go into the houses without windows, because of the smell. Still, she did so, because she knew the people needed her love and care.

Some of Elizabeth's friends joined her in her work with the poor. They formed a group called the Society for the Relief of Poor Widows and Small Children. In addition to caring for the poor, the "Widows' Society" sewed clothes for them and raised money to help them.

Other women who knew Elizabeth couldn't believe that she and her friends would work in the filthy slums. They really disliked the idea of coming into contact with the poor people. Still, the women in the "Widows' Society" continued with their work in spite of the disapproval of others.

When William's father died, William's younger brothers and sisters came to live with him, Elizabeth, and their children. This extra responsibility for Elizabeth and William was not always easy. Elizabeth now had more children to care for. William had to run the shipping business alone. They worked very hard. In addition to her own work, Elizabeth helped William as much as she could.

At that time, many people were coming to the United States from other countries, seeking a better life. These people came by boat and landed in New York City. The voyage was very long, and the travelers often became sick. They also brought diseases, some of them very serious, to New York. Elizabeth's father, Dr. Bayley, was made Inspector General of the Health Department. Hoping to help stop the spread of these diseases, Dr. Bayley set up a medical station on Staten Island (an island just off the New York coast). The immigrants who were sick or carrying disease stayed at the medical station until they were well. One of the serious diseases that the immigrants brought with them was yellow fever. Dr. Bayley became very sick with this disease and died.

During this same time, a war broke out between England and France. The war hurt the shipping business. Pirates captured several of the Seton ships. These ships carried valuable items that would bring money. Without this money, the Seton shipping business was in trouble. William had much to worry about. Even though he worked very hard, he finally had to close the business. The worry and hard work had weakened William's health, and he became very sick with tuberculosis. Tuberculosis is a disease that usually damages the lungs. William had a fever, and he coughed a lot. He lost his desire for food and began to lose weight. There was no medicine that could help cure tuberculosis. William's doctor suggested that he go to Italy to live with friends; there, it was usually sunny and William could get a lot of rest.

William, Elizabeth, and their eldest daughter, Annina, set off by ship for Italy. There, they were planning to stay with William's friends, the Filicchis. The other Seton children remained in New York with relatives.

The voyage to Italy took many days. Annina became sick with whooping cough, a very serious disease, and William suffered a great deal with his tuberculosis. Elizabeth spent her time nursing them, looking forward to their arrival in Italy. But because William was so sick, they were not allowed to travel to the home of the Filicchis. Instead, Elizabeth, William, and Annina were required to go to a place called the Lazaretto. It reminded Elizabeth of the hospital where the sick immigrants to the United States stayed. The Lazaretto was not a hospital, however. It was a cold, stone building set on an island. Here, the Setons stayed for almost a month, in a room with no furnishings other than three mattresses.

It was a cold and damp place, and the Setons had only a small fire to warm themselves. The Filicchis sent them food, blankets, cough syrups, and liquids to drink. Elizabeth spent the days reading the Bible and teaching Annina, as well as caring for William. Finally, the Setons were given permission to leave the Lazaretto. But soon afterward, before they could get to the Filicchis, William died from the tuberculosis.

Elizabeth and Annina were filled with sorrow when William died, and Elizabeth felt very lonely. The Filicchi family brought Elizabeth and Annina to live with them. Though Elizabeth was Protestant, she chose to attend Mass with the Filicchis, who were Catholic. In the Catholic Church Elizabeth found peace, and she had a great desire to learn more about the Catholic faith. She began to read about the saints and to study the Catholic faith. Elizabeth took comfort from the idea of Mary's being her Mother in heaven.

Elizabeth and Annina stayed in Italy for several months and then returned to New York. Elizabeth was so happy to see her other children again. Soon after her arrival home, Elizabeth decided to join the Catholic Church. Most of her relatives and friends were very upset with her when she made this decision, and they did not want to have anything to do with her or her children. This rejection was hard on Elizabeth and hurt her very much, but she and her children still chose to join the Catholic Church.

Elizabeth now needed to raise money to support her family. She found a job teaching school. The Filicchis and a long-time friend of Elizabeth's sent money to help her, also. Elizabeth was very grateful to God and her friends for their help.

It was a very difficult time for Elizabeth. Some people were so upset with Elizabeth's decision to become a Catholic that they were often cruel and rude to her. They spread rumors and lies about her. Some people even demanded that Elizabeth and her children leave New York. This is exactly what they did when, in this difficult time, Elizabeth received an invitation from the bishop in Baltimore, Maryland. He wanted Elizabeth to open a Catholic school there. Elizabeth and her children went to Baltimore. They lived and taught school in a two-story house. Children came from all parts of the town. The townspeople were fond of Elizabeth and treated her with great respect.

Soon, some young women joined Elizabeth in her work, teaching the children in the Catholic school. They also cared for the poor and the sick. With permission from the bishop, Elizabeth and the young women formed a religious community, the Daughters of Charity. The religious habit they wore was a long black dress, a short black cape, and a white cap that tied with a black bow. As the head of the new religious order, Elizabeth was now known as Mother Seton.

Elizabeth's daughters remained with her, and her sons went away to school. William's sisters, Harriet and Cecilia, came to live with Elizabeth. They too had joined the Catholic Church.

There were so many children coming to their school that a new school building had to be built. A generous man provided the money to build a new school, as well as a home for the sisters to live in. Elizabeth, her daughters, and the Daughters of Charity had to travel by covered wagon and by foot to the spot chosen for the new school. They had very few possessions to take with them, for they were very poor. Among these few items were statues of Mary and Saint Vincent de Paul.

When they arrived at the site for the new school, there was only an old log house for them to live in. Some of the windows did not have any glass, and the house needed to be cleaned. It was not an easy or comfortable life for them.

Finally, the new school and a new house made of stone were completed. There, the sisters taught the many children—wealthy and poor—who came to them.

The Daughters of Charity continued to grow as more young women wished to join the community. But there was little food to eat, and the

Daughters' new stone house could be cold, especially when wind and rain blew in through the cracks of the walls. William's sister Harriet became very ill and died. Her sister Cecilia died just five months later. Elizabeth was very sad to lose two people she loved so much.

Elizabeth continued with her work, though, and over time a new, larger home and school were built. The home and school were large enough so that the Daughters of Charity could now open a boarding school where the students would live, as well as attend school. More than a hundred girls were enrolled in the boarding school. The sisters cared for them and provided them with food, a place to sleep, and lots of love. Some people were not able to pay to send their children to the boarding school, so the sisters opened a free school as well.

Soon, Elizabeth was to experience more grief. Her eldest daughter, Annina, became very ill with tuberculosis. Annina wanted to become a Daughter of Charity, and this she was allowed to do several days before she died. Elizabeth arranged to have her buried next to William's sisters.

Not long after, Elizabeth's youngest daughter, Rebecca, also became ill with tuberculosis, after suffering from a broken hip and an injured knee. Rebecca died in her mother's arms, and the youngest daughter was buried beside the eldest.

Elizabeth suffered patiently and worked hard tending the school and the growing religious community. Three years after their community was established, the Daughters of Charity received formal confirmation of their order from the archbishop. Their religious garments remained the same black dress and cape, with a black cap replacing the white one.

Over the years, Elizabeth saw the Daughters of Charity grow. They opened a hospital in Philadelphia and an orphanage in New York City. Everywhere they went, they taught school and cared for the poor and sick.

Elizabeth died of tuberculosis on January 4, 1821, at the age of forty-six. She was the first person born in the United States to be declared a saint by the Catholic Church. She was declared a saint on September 14, 1975. Her feast day is January 4.

What of Elizabeth's three other children? Her daughter Catherine became a Sister of Mercy. Her son Richard died at sea after saving the life of a minister. Her son William married, and one of his children became an archbishop in the Catholic Church.

Elizabeth Ann Seton showed her love for God and others by following Jesus and the Ten Commandments in spite of the many hardships she suffered. Elizabeth cared for the homeless and the elderly, she nursed the sick, and she educated many children. Her work is still carried on today by the Daughters of Charity.

God wants us to become saints, too. We can become saints by loving and following Jesus, by following the Ten Commandments, and by acting as images of God. We can follow the example of Saint Elizabeth Ann Seton.

Saint Elizabeth Ann Seton showed her love for God and others by following Jesus and the Ten Commandments in spite of the many hardships she suffered. Write down three ways that Saint Elizabeth Ann Seton showed her love for God and others by following Jesus and the Ten Commandments.

1 _____

_____

_____

2 _____

_____

_____

3 _____

_____

_____

We can imitate Saint Elizabeth Ann Seton and show our love for God and others by following Jesus and the Ten Commandments in spite of the difficult things we might experience in our lives. What are three ways that you can imitate Saint Elizabeth Ann Seton?

1 _____

_____

_____

2 _____

_____

_____

3 _____

_____

_____

Read the following stories. Decide which commandment applies and if the commandment is being followed. Then state how the commandment is or is not being followed. Write your answers in the space provided.

1 Daniel's room is a mess. His mom tells him to clean it. He gets angry and yells at her. Daniel tells his mom that he doesn't have to clean up his room and that no one can make him clean his room.
Which commandment applies to this story? _____
Is the commandment being followed? _____
Explain:

_____

_____

_____

_____

_____

2 Kevin has two brothers, and you have two sisters. Kevin's brothers are always playing sports with him. You wish you could trade your two sisters for Kevin's brothers, so you would have someone to play sports with.
Which commandment applies to this story? _____
Is the commandment being followed? _____
Explain:

_____

_____

_____

3 When you change your clothes in your room, you always close the door. When the bathroom door is closed and you want to use the room, you always knock to make sure no one is there.
Which commandment applies to this story? _____
Is the commandment being followed? _____
Explain:

_____

_____

_____

4 Your friends want you to go to the store with them. You tell them you don't have any money. They say that's no problem; they will show you how to take what you want without paying for it. You think this is a neat idea and go along with them. There are some things you've been wanting from the store. When you get to the store, you take and hide something in your pocket. You leave the store without paying for the item you took.

Which commandment applies to this story? _____

Is the commandment being followed? _____

Explain:

_____

_____

_____

_____

5 Joe tells you an untrue story about the new girl in school. You tell him that you don't believe the story and that he shouldn't tell the story to anyone else.

Which commandment applies to this story? _____

Is the commandment being followed? _____

Explain:

_____

_____

_____

6 Sarah is fifteen years old, and she just found out she is going to have a baby. She has heard that an abortion can solve this problem, but Sarah doesn't want to hurt her unborn baby. Even though she is very scared, Sarah tells her parents what has happened. Sarah tells her parents that she wants to have the baby. After the baby is born, she will make an adoption plan for the baby. Sarah's parents support Sarah's right decision.

Which commandment applies to this story? _____

Is the commandment being followed? _____

Explain:

_____

_____

_____

7 Karen's friend Amy just got a new bike. Karen's bike belonged to her older sister. It's not bright and shiny like Amy's new bike. Karen really likes Amy's new bike, but Karen is still happy with the bike she has.

Which commandment applies to this story? _____

Is the commandment being followed? _____

Explain:

_____

_____

_____

_____

8 The playground supervisor told Stephanie that she had to go in from recess because she was not obeying the playground rules. Stephanie is really angry with the playground supervisor and decides to tell lies. She tells her parents that the playground supervisor is mean and calls her names. Stephanie wants the playground supervisor to get into trouble, so she makes up these lies.

Which commandment applies to this story? _____

Is the commandment being followed? _____

Explain:

_____

_____

_____

_____

9 You find a completed page of homework without a name on it. You have not done that page, and you don't want to do it. You put your name on the page you found and hand it in as your own.

Which commandment applies to this story? _____

Is the commandment being followed? _____

Explain:

_____

_____

_____

_____

10 Mike knows his mom has had a hard day at work, so he does the dishes for her so she can rest after supper.
Which commandment applies to this story? _____
Is the commandment being followed? _____
Explain:

_____

_____

_____

_____

_____

11 Bob and Ellen love each other very much, but they aren't sure they want to get married. They decide they will live together first.
Which commandment applies to this story? _____
Is the commandment being followed? _____
Explain:

_____

_____

_____

_____

_____

12 Jenny's friends pressure her to try some drugs with them, but Jenny says no.
Which commandment applies to this story? _____
Is the commandment being followed? _____
Explain:

_____

_____

_____

_____

_____

18

We Pray

What is prayer?
Prayer is talking with God.

What are the four kinds of prayer?
Adoration
Thanksgiving
Petition
Contrition

What are prayers of adoration?
Prayers in which we praise God for His power, wisdom, and love.

What are prayers of thanksgiving?
Prayers in which we tell God "thank you" for all He has given us.

What are prayers of petition?
Prayers in which we ask God for the things we need.

What are prayers of contrition?
Prayers in which we tell God we are sorry for our sins and ask
Him to forgive us.

In prayers of petition, whom may we ask to intercede for us?
We may ask the saints and angels to intercede for us and bring our
petitions to God.

*You can speak and confide in Him; you can address Him with
affection and confidence.*

POPE JOHN PAUL II

Vocabulary

intercede: to ask for something on behalf of someone else.

What is Prayer?

Prayer is talking with God. When we pray, we raise our minds and hearts to God. We can pray anytime and anywhere. Sometimes we talk privately to God, using our own words and telling Him what we are thinking about. This can take place anytime. A quick conversation with God can also happen anywhere—in gym, on the playground, in a living room. When we are trying to have a longer talk with God, it is sometimes better to find a quiet place, where we will not be interrupted—such as a bedroom or a chapel.

We can pray alone or with other people. When we pray, we should take time to be quiet and to listen to God. He speaks to us in our hearts.

We know that prayer is our way of talking with God and sharing the events of our lives with Him. Sometimes we pray for a long time, telling God many things. Other times we say very short prayers, telling God about one specific thing. There are different kinds of prayers we can say to God. We can say prayers praising God for His power, wisdom, and love. We can say prayers telling God "thank you" for all that He gives to us. We can ask God for the things that we need. We can ask the saints and angels to bring our petitions to God for us. We can tell God that we are sorry for our wrong choices and ask Him to forgive us.

God always hears and answers our prayers. God does not always answer our prayers in a way we would like them to be answered. Rather, God answers our prayers in a way that He knows is best for us. When our prayers are not answered the way we want them to be, or when we need strength to do something that is hard for us to do, we should pray to God the Father the way that Jesus did in the Garden of Gethsemane: "Not my will but yours be done" (Luke 22:42). Remember, God the Holy Spirit is always with us to help us and to give us strength.

Prayer is a conversation with God. When we pray, we raise our minds and hearts to God. We talk to God.

Why must we pray?

We must pray first because we are believers. We come from God, we belong to God, and we return to God.

We must pray . . . because we are weak and guilty.

—Prayer gives strength;
—Prayer gives courage;
—Prayer gives light.

Therefore, do not stop praying! Let not a day pass without having prayed a little!

Prayer is a duty, but it is also a great joy, because it is a conversation with God through Jesus Christ!
    —Pope John Paul II

Kinds of Prayer

There are four different kinds of prayer: adoration, thanksgiving, petition, and contrition.

Adoration: Prayers of adoration are prayers in which we praise God for His power, wisdom, and love. One example of a prayer of adoration is the *Gloria*, which we pray or sing together at Mass. In the *Gloria*, we give praise to the Holy Trinity.

Gloria

Glory to God in the highest,
and peace to his people on earth.

Lord God, heavenly King,
almighty God and Father,
   we worship you, we give you thanks,
   we praise you for your glory.

Lord Jesus Christ, only Son of the Father,
Lord God, Lamb of God,
you take away the sin of the world:
   have mercy on us;
you are seated at the right hand of the Father:
   receive our prayer.

For you alone are the Holy One,
you alone are the Lord,
you alone are the Most High,
   Jesus Christ,
   with the Holy Spirit,
   in the glory of God the Father. Amen.

Thanksgiving: In prayers of thanksgiving, we tell God "thank you" for all that He gives us. We should remember that it is God Who gives us all that we need, and we should thank Him.

One prayer that we say to thank God for all of His gifts is the "Grace after Meals".

Grace after Meals

We give You thanks for all Your benefits, O Almighty God,
Who lives and reigns forever. Amen.

There are many Psalms (prayers) in the Bible that give thanks to God. The following prayer is based on Psalm 138, written by the Hebrew King David, who lived many years before the time of Christ.

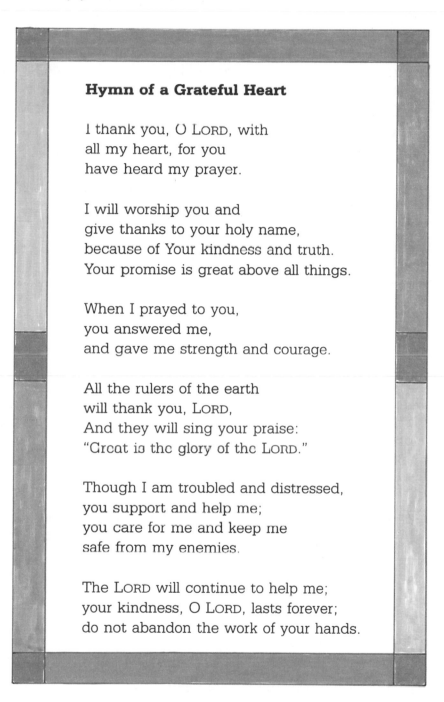

Hymn of a Grateful Heart

I thank you, O LORD, with
all my heart, for you
have heard my prayer.

I will worship you and
give thanks to your holy name,
because of Your kindness and truth.
Your promise is great above all things.

When I prayed to you,
you answered me,
and gave me strength and courage.

All the rulers of the earth
will thank you, LORD,
And they will sing your praise:
"Great is the glory of the LORD."

Though I am troubled and distressed,
you support and help me;
you care for me and keep me
safe from my enemies.

The LORD will continue to help me;
your kindness, O LORD, lasts forever;
do not abandon the work of your hands.

Petition: Prayers of petition are prayers in which we ask God for the things we need, and we also pray for the needs of others. For example, we pray prayers of petition at Mass. We pray for the needs of the Church, for government leaders, for the salvation of the world, for the needy, and for people in our community.

While Jesus was on earth, He told the Apostles, "Do not let your hearts be troubled. You have faith in God; have faith also in me" (John 14:1). He also told the people, "Come to me, all you who labor and are burdened, and I will give you rest" (Matthew 11:28). After Jesus ascended into heaven, Saint Peter told the early Christians, "Cast all your worries upon him because he cares for you" (1 Peter 5:7).

We can bring our petitions to God any time. We can bring our petitions to God through the saints and angels. When we ask the saints and angels to bring our petitions to God for us, we are asking them to intercede for us with God. The saints and angels do not grant petitions, but they take our petitions to God and ask Him to grant them. We can ask Mary, the Mother of God, to help us by her prayers. One prayer we can pray to Mary is called the *Memorare*. In the *Memorare* we ask Mary to help us.

The Memorare

Remember, O most gracious Virgin Mary,
that never was it known
that anyone who fled to thy protection,
implored thy help,
or sought thy intercession,
was left unaided.
Inspired with this confidence,
I fly unto thee,
O Virgin of virgins, my mother.
To thee I come;
before thee I stand, sinful and sorrowful.
O Mother of the Word Incarnate,
despise not my petitions,
but, in thy mercy, hear and answer me. Amen.

Contrition: In a prayer of contrition, we tell God we are sorry for our sins and ask Him to forgive us. When we say a prayer of contrition, we tell God we are sorry for our sins because we have hurt Him, ourselves, and others, and that with His help we will try not to sin again. It is a good idea to make an act of contrition each day.

An Act of Contrition

My God,
I am sorry for my sins with all my heart.
In choosing to do wrong and failing to do good,
I have sinned against you,
    Whom I should love above all things.
I have hurt myself and others.
I firmly intend, with your help, to do penance,
    to sin no more, and to avoid whatever leads me to sin.
Our Savior Jesus Christ suffered and died for us.
In His name, my God, have mercy.

Read the following sentences. Write the missing words in the spaces provided. The words are hidden in the "Word Find". As you complete each statement, find and circle the hidden words in the diagram.

- In a prayer of _____, we tell God "thank you" for all He has given us.

- A prayer of _____ tells God we are sorry for our sins and asks Him to forgive us.

- When we pray we raise our _____ and _____ to God.

- In a prayer of _____, we praise and honor God.

- _____ is talking with God.

- In prayers of _____, we ask God for the things we need.

WORD FIND

```
G  S  P  Q  H  E  A  R  T  S  R  M  M  N  X  Y  Z
A  V  N  B  R  C  D  O  O  T  Y  X  X  P  E  W  N
P  C  M  U  U  S  O  A  N  P  E  T  I  E  M  I  N
O  O  R  A  T  P  R  A  Y  E  R  M  I  T  V  X  E
I  N  B  P  R  A  A  X  T  L  L  S  M  I  N  D  S
W  T  B  T  S  I  T  H  E  A  N  D  S  T  T  S  W
S  R  P  O  V  N  I  X  T  Y  Y  L  D  I  N  J  H
H  I  T  R  W  W  O  R  N  D  F  L  P  O  O  I  M
S  T  Q  T  H  A  N  K  S  G  I  V  I  N  G  B  B
P  I  T  I  O  J  G  M  L  R  W  P  Z  X  S  D  H
G  O  O  D  L  O  V  A  S  T  H  G  Y  R  S  T  P
A  N  B  D  K  L  C  E  I  W  T  O  X  H  G  Z  Y
```

Write your own prayers—one of each kind:

Prayer of Adoration

_____

_____

_____

_____

Prayer of Thanksgiving

_____

_____

_____

_____

Prayer of Petition

_____

_____

_____

_____

Prayer of Contrition

_____

_____

_____

_____

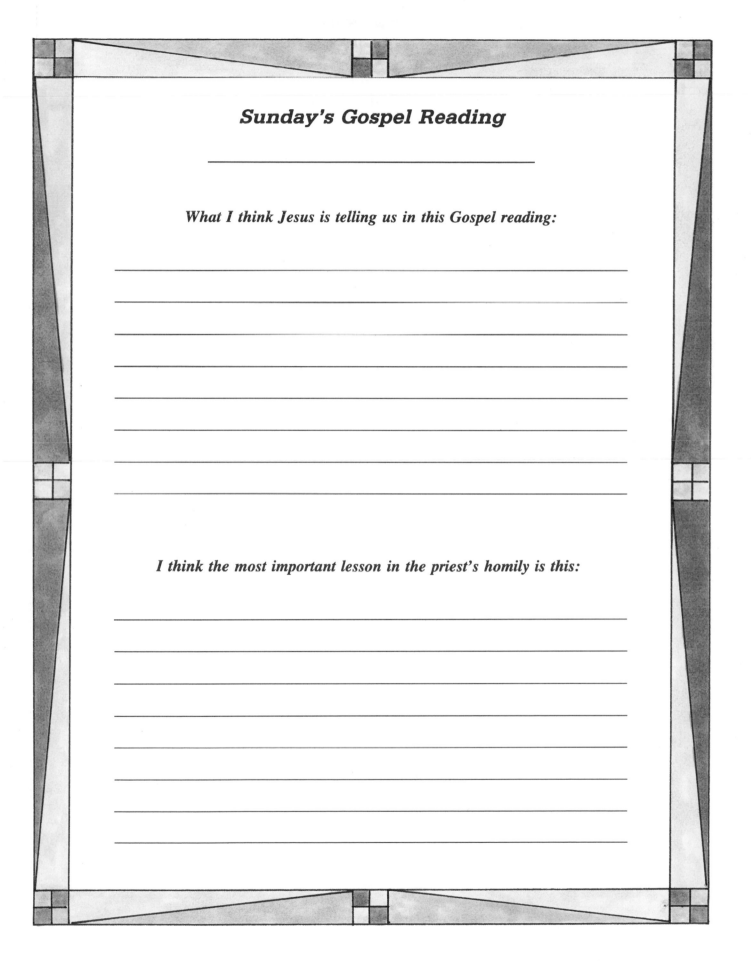

Sunday's Gospel Reading

_____

What I think Jesus is telling us in this Gospel reading:

_____

_____

_____

_____

_____

_____

_____

I think the most important lesson in the priest's homily is this:

_____

_____

_____

_____

_____

_____

_____

_____

19

Mary,
the Mother of God

God gave Mary a special gift. From the very first moment of her life, Mary was without sin. In other words, from the very first moment of her life, Mary shared God's life, grace. What is this special privilege to Mary called?
Her Immaculate Conception.

The angel Gabriel was sent by God to ask Mary to be the Mother of God the Son, Jesus. What is this event called?
The Annunciation.

Mary traveled many miles to visit her cousin Elizabeth, who was soon to give birth to her baby. Mary wanted to help Elizabeth and care for her. What is this event called?
The Visitation.

Jesus brought Mary, body and soul, into heaven. What is this event called?
The Assumption.

What are the Joyful Mysteries of the Rosary?
Annunciation
Visitation
Birth of Jesus
Presentation
Finding the Child Jesus in the Temple

What are the Sorrowful Mysteries of the Rosary?
Agony in the Garden
Scourging at the Pillar
Crowning with Thorns
Carrying of the Cross
Crucifixion

Continues

What are the Glorious Mysteries of the Rosary?
Resurrection
Ascension
Descent of the Holy Spirit
Assumption of Mary
Coronation of Mary as Queen of Heaven and Earth

What are the Holy Days of obligation in the United States?
Solemnity of Mary, Mother of God—January 1
Ascension—forty days after Easter
Assumption—August 15
All Saints' Day—November 1
Immaculate Conception—December 8
Christmas—December 25

Under the cross, Mary's spiritual motherhood reached its key moment. Jesus linked her, then, with every man, as He united her afterwards with the Church on Pentecost. From that day, the whole Church had her as Mother, and all men have her as Mother.

POPE JOHN PAUL II

Vocabulary

Holy Days of obligation: days on which the Church celebrates certain events in the lives of Jesus and Mary, and on which the Church honors the saints. We should go to Mass on Holy Days.

Mary, conceived without sin, pray for us who have recourse to thee.

God Chose Mary

God the Father chose a young woman to be the Mother of His Son, Jesus. This woman was Mary.

God chose Saint Ann and Saint Joachim to be Mary's parents. Ann and Joachim were very holy, devout, and charitable people. They shared what they had with the poor. Ann and Joachim prayed and asked God to bless them with a child. Mary was born to Ann and Joachim. The Church celebrates the birth of Mary on September 8.

God gave Mary a special gift. From the very first moment of her life, Mary was without sin. In other words, from the first moment of her life, Mary shared God's life, grace. This special privilege given to Mary is called her Immaculate Conception.

The Church celebrates the feast of the Immaculate Conception on December 8. This is a Holy Day of obligation, and we go to Mass.

Mary loved her parents and did not cause them any trouble. Filled with God's grace, Mary was a very holy and devout child. Mary never sinned—she was always full of grace. Mary had a great love for God. Her great love for God was reflected in all that she thought, said, and did. Mary showed her love for God through her life of prayer, sacrifice, compassion, and charity.

Hail, Mary, full of grace, the Lord is with you.

The Annunciation

When Mary was about fourteen years old, she was engaged to marry a man named Joseph. God sent a messenger, the angel Gabriel, to ask Mary to be the Mother of the Savior.

The angel Gabriel said to Mary, "Hail, favored one! The Lord is with you" (Luke 1:28). Mary didn't understand Gabriel's greeting and wondered what it meant. Gabriel told Mary not to be afraid. He said, "Behold, you will conceive in your womb and bear a son, and you shall name him Jesus. He will be great and will be called Son of the Most High . . ."

Mary asked how this could happen. The angel Gabriel explained to Mary that it would happen through the power of the Holy Spirit, and that nothing is impossible with God.

Mary said, "Behold, I am the handmaid of the Lord. May it be done to me according to your word." Then the angel left her.

Mary believed what the angel told her and was willing to do God's will. Mary said "yes" to God.

—based on Luke 1:28–38

This event in Mary's life is called the Annunciation. The Church celebrates the Annunciation on March 25.

An angel also spoke to Joseph in a dream. The angel told him: "Joseph, son of David, do not be afraid to take Mary your wife into your home. For it is through the holy Spirit that this child has been conceived in her. She will bear a son and you are to name him Jesus, because he will save his people from their sins" (Matthew 1:20–21). When Joseph awoke, he did as the angel of the Lord had instructed him in the dream.

Blessed are you among women, and blessed is the fruit of your womb, Jesus.

The Visitation

The angel Gabriel had also told Mary that her cousin Elizabeth was going to have a baby. Mary loved Elizabeth and wanted to help her. Mary traveled the long distance (about eighty miles) to Elizabeth's house. When

Mary arrived, she greeted Elizabeth. Elizabeth was filled with joy from God and said to Mary, "Most blessed are you among women, and blessed is the fruit of your womb. And how does this happen to me, that the mother of my Lord should come to me? For at the moment the sound of your greeting reached my ears, the infant in my womb leaped for joy. Blessed are you who believed that what was spoken to you by the Lord would be fulfilled" (Luke 1:42–45).

After Elizabeth greeted Mary, Mary praised God with a beautiful prayer called the "Canticle of Mary", or the "Magnificat". Mary stayed with Elizabeth for about three months. Mary helped Elizabeth and cared for her.

This event in Mary's life is called the Visitation. The Church celebrates the Visitation on May 31.

For today in the city of David a savior has been born for you who is Messiah and Lord.
        —Luke 2:11

The Nativity

Mary returned home to Nazareth. She and Joseph began their married life together and prepared for the time when Jesus would be born.

The Roman government was taking a census and counting all the people in the land. Mary and Joseph had to travel to Bethlehem to register and be counted. When they reached the town of Bethlehem, Mary told Joseph that the time had come for her baby to be born. All of the inns were filled. The only place Joseph could find for them to stay was in a stable. It was there that Jesus, God the Son, was born. Mary gently wrapped Him in swaddling clothes and placed Him in a manger.

Out in the fields, shepherds were tending their flocks. Angels brought them wonderful news of the Savior's birth. The shepherds went to the stable where the Holy Family was. There, they knelt before Jesus, their Savior, and they praised God. Wise men from other countries also came to honor Jesus and to bring Him gifts. The Church celebrates the birth of Jesus on December 25—Christmas. Christmas is a Holy Day of obligation. We go to Mass on Christmas to honor Jesus on His birthday.

The Church honors Mary as the Mother of God. The Church celebrates this day on January 1—the Solemnity of Mary, Mother of God. This is a Holy Day of obligation. We go to Mass on this day to honor Mary, the Mother of God, and our heavenly Mother.

When Jesus was still a baby, Mary and Joseph took Him to the temple in Jerusalem. They brought the baby Jesus to the temple to present Him to God and to pray. This was the custom of the Jewish people. When a very holy man named Simeon saw Jesus, he gave thanks to God for allowing him to see the Savior of the world. Simeon told Mary things that would happen in the future, and he blessed her. This event is called the Presentation. The Church celebrates the Presentation on February 2.

After a while, King Herod was looking for Jesus to kill Him. Jesus, Mary, and Joseph had to flee to Egypt in order to keep Jesus safe from King Herod. The journey to Egypt was long and hard. They lived in Egypt until Herod died and it was safe for them to return to Nazareth.

And Jesus advanced [in] wisdom and age and favor before God and man.
—Luke 2:52

The Holy Family

The Holy Family made their home in Nazareth. Joseph worked as a carpenter. Mary took care of the house and spent many hours in prayer. Jesus helped both Joseph and Mary.

When Jesus was twelve, Mary and Joseph took Him to Jerusalem to celebrate the Jewish feast of Passover. After the Passover, all of their friends and relatives, together with other people, started the long journey home. Mary and Joseph thought that Jesus was among the travelers, walking with His friends. They searched through the crowd and asked if anyone knew where Jesus was. Mary and Joseph were worried when they couldn't find Jesus. Immediately they started back to Jerusalem to search for Him. Three days went by before they found Him. He was in the temple. Jesus was talking to scholars who had studied about God and knew about Him. These men were amazed at how intelligent and wise Jesus was for his age. Mary and Joseph were very happy when they found Jesus. They thanked God for helping them to find Jesus. The Holy Family returned home together, and Jesus obeyed Mary and Joseph.

Mary said to them, "Do whatever he tells you."
        —John 2:5

The Miracle at Cana

When Jesus was thirty years old, He was baptized in the Jordan River by John the Baptist (Zechariah and Elizabeth's son). Jesus went to the desert to fast and pray, and then He began calling His disciples.

Jesus, Mary, and Jesus' disciples were invited to a wedding in Cana. When the wine ran out during the banquet, Mary went to Jesus and told Him what had happened. Jesus said to her, "Woman, how does your concern affect me? My hour has not yet come" (John 2:4). Mary told the waiters, "Do whatever he tells you" (John 2:5). Jesus told the waiters to fill six stone jars with water. Then Jesus performed His first miracle and changed the water into wine.

Jesus spent the following three years teaching, forgiving, and healing the people.

Jesus said to Mary, "Woman, behold, your son."
        —John 19:26

Mary, Our Mother

At the end of the Gospels, we see Mary at the foot of the Cross. Of course, Mary saw Jesus during the three years He spent teaching people about God, healing them, and forgiving their sins. Also, the Stations of the Cross tell us that Jesus met His Mother as He carried the Cross to the place where He was crucified. Mary was with Jesus when He died—she stood at the foot of the Cross and shared in her Son's pain, suffering, and sorrow. As Mary stood at the foot of the Cross, Jesus saw her. His disciple John also was there. Jesus said to Mary, "Woman, behold, your son" (John 19:26). Then Jesus said to John, "Behold, your mother" (John 19:27). John cared for Mary from that time on.

Christ's death is called the Crucifixion. The Church remembers Jesus' death on the Cross at every Mass and on Good Friday.

Holy Mary, Mother of God, pray for us sinners.

Mary, Mother of the Church

Jesus rose from the dead on Easter Sunday. This is called His Resurrection. Of course, Jesus must have spent time with Mary after His Resurrection. Forty days afterward, Jesus ascended into heaven. This is called the Ascension. We celebrate the Resurrection on Easter Sunday. We celebrate the Ascension forty days after Easter. The Ascension is a Holy Day of obligation.

We next hear of Mary at the time of Pentecost. On Pentecost, Mary was with the Apostles when God the Holy Spirit came to them. The Holy Spirit was sent by God the Father and God the Son to strengthen the Apostles, to fill them with grace and joy, and to guide the Church.

Because Mary accepted God's invitation to be the Mother of the Messiah, we honor her as Mother of the Church, which Jesus established to carry on His work on earth.

Pope John Paul II tells us:

So, love our Lady, dear children!
Pray to her every day!
May the Blessed Virgin, prayed to, loved and imitated,
help you to remain good and happy in a holy way!

And you, my dearest friends,
remember well these words
which the Mother of Christ spoke at Cana,
turning to those who were to fill the water jars.

She said then, pointing to her Son,
"Do whatever he tells you!" (John 2:5).

To you also she says the same thing today.

Accept these words.
Remember them.
Put them into practice.

Mary has appeared to people is different places around the world, telling them of her love for all people. Mary wishes to help all people. The following stories are about two of Mary's appearances. Mary appeared to a man named Juan Diego in a place called Guadalupe, in Mexico. Mary also appeared to a young girl named Bernadette Soubirous, in Lourdes, France.

Our Lady of Guadalupe

IN the year 1531, the Spaniards were in charge of the government of Mexico. The relationship between the Indians and the Spaniards was not good, and the Indians were thinking of attacking the Spaniards.

The bishop of Mexico, Juan de Zumarraga, knew that it would take a miracle to prevent a revolt. Being devoted to the Blessed Virgin Mary, he implored her help.

Mary chose an Aztec Indian called Juan Diego to bring the people the message of God's love. Juan, his wife, and his uncle had become members of the Catholic Church a few years earlier, in 1525. When Juan's wife died, he moved to the town of Tolpetlac, where he lived with his uncle.

On the morning of December 9, 1531, long before sunrise, Juan Diego rose from his bed. He was going to attend the Saturday morning Mass, and he began the long walk from Tolpetlac to church. It was a walk he made every morning. Dawn had just broken as he neared the hill of Tepeyac. From the top of the hill came a beautiful, melodious song, as if from many different birds. Juan, looking up, saw a glittering cloud, dazzling white. From the center of the cloud came a radiant, bright light. The rays of light formed a brilliant rainbow around the cloud. Juan was filled with a sense of great peace and happiness. Suddenly it became very quiet, and then Juan heard a woman's voice calling him. He rushed up the hill. There in front of the dazzling white cloud stood the most beautiful young woman Juan had ever seen. Her clothing cast such a bright light that the rocks gleamed like precious gems, the leaves on the cactus resembled clusters of emeralds, and the trunks and branches were like gold. Even the ground was transformed. Juan knelt down before the Lady. She spoke to him in his own language: "My son, Juan Diego, where are you going?" Juan explained that he was on his way to Mass. Then she said to him, "You must know and be very certain in your heart, my son, that I am truly the perpetual and perfect Virgin Mary, holy Mother of the True God through whom everything lives, the Creator and Master of Heaven and Earth."

Mary went on to tell Juan that she wanted a chapel built, where she would show and give all her love, compassion, help, and protection to the people. Mary told Juan that she was his merciful Mother, the Mother of all the people living in Mexico, and the Mother of all people everywhere. She was the Mother of all people who love her, implore her, seek her, and trust her. Mary told Juan that she would respond to their sorrow and would help them.

Mary told Juan to go and see the Bishop of Mexico. Juan was to tell the bishop that Mary had sent him with the message that a chapel be built in the place where she had appeared. Juan was to tell the bishop all he had seen and heard. Juan bowed to Mary and promised to do as she asked. He set out immediately to see the bishop.

At sunset on the same day, after having seen the bishop, Juan returned to the hill of Tepeyac. The Blessed Virgin Mary stood where she had in the morning and waited to hear Juan's report. Juan fell to his knees at her feet and cried, "My beautiful Lady, my Queen, my Love, I went where you sent me." Juan told Mary that it had been very difficult for him to obtain a meeting with the bishop. Juan said that the bishop had welcomed him and listened to all he had to say, but Juan felt that the bishop didn't believe him. The bishop had promised to think over what Juan had told him and asked Juan to come back another day, when he would have more time to talk.

Juan pleaded with Mary to send a well-known, important person to speak for her. He felt the bishop would believe a more important person. Juan was a poor man, and he feared that he was not worthy of this task. Then Juan begged Mary to forgive him, for he did not want to hurt or displease her.

The Blessed Virgin Mary said to Juan Diego, "Most beloved son, you know that there are many servants I could send to carry out my orders if that were my desire, but it is necessary that through your intervention my desire be fulfilled, and so I beg you, my son, and order you to return again tomorrow and see the bishop and tell him once again that it is the perpetual Virgin, Holy Mary, the Mother of God who sends you to him."

Again, Juan promised to deliver the message to the bishop and to return the next afternoon with the bishop's answer. Juan wanted so much to please Mary, but deep in his heart he feared he would not be allowed to see the bishop. And even if he were to see the bishop, he wondered if the bishop would believe him.

The following morning, December 10, Juan Diego went to church for Sunday Mass. After Mass was over, Juan walked to the bishop's house. After hours of difficulty with the guards, Juan was allowed to see the bishop again. Juan told the bishop that he had seen Mary the Mother of God in the same place a second time. Juan explained that Mary had waited for the bishop's reply to her message, and that Mary had sent Juan once more to let the bishop know that he must build her a chapel. This chapel was to be built in the place where Juan had seen Mary and spoken to her. Juan repeated that it was the Mother of God, the everlasting Virgin Mary, who commanded it.

The bishop listened intently to Juan and began to believe what he was saying. The bishop questioned him repeatedly. The bishop told Juan that his

word alone was not enough for the bishop to act on. Juan must ask the Lady to give a sign, some proof, showing that she was the Mother of God and that it was her will to have the chapel built for her.

Juan believed that Mary would give him the necessary proof to bring to the bishop. On his way home, Juan returned to the hill of Tepeyac. There he found the Virgin Mary waiting for him. Juan told Mary that he had repeated her message to the bishop and answered all the questions the bishop had asked about her. The bishop believed Juan, but because this was a serious matter, the bishop requested a sign or token from the Blessed Virgin Mary. Juan told Mary he had promised to accept whatever sign she was pleased to give him and joyfully take it to the bishop. Mary thanked Juan for carrying out her requests and then said, "Tomorrow, Juan, my son, you will see me, and I will give you the sign that will assure him. No longer will he doubt or be suspicious of you. Be sure, my son, that you will be compensated for all the trouble, work, and fatigue that you have suffered for me. Go in peace; tomorrow I will be waiting for you here."

Upon arriving home that evening, Juan found his uncle deathly ill. Immediately, Juan went to get a doctor for his uncle. The doctor gave Juan some medicine for his uncle and left. Juan gave his uncle the medicine, but it didn't help. Juan's uncle, fearing he would die, asked to have a priest come to hear his confession. Early on the morning of December 12, Juan left to get the priest. Juan was so worried, he completely forgot about his meeting with the Blessed Virgin Mary. Juan was deep in thought as he approached Tepeyac hill. Suddenly, he looked up and saw the Blessed Virgin Mary walking down the hill toward him. Feeling sad, ashamed, and frightened, Juan approached slowly, bowed to Mary, and greeted her. Mary asked Juan where he was going and why he had taken another road.

Juan explained that his uncle was dying and that he was going to get the priest. Juan promised to go to the bishop as soon as he had taken the priest to his uncle. Mary replied, "Listen and be sure, my dear son, that I will protect you; do not be frightened or grieve, or let your heart be dismayed, however great your uncle's illness may be that you speak of. Am I not here? I, who am your Mother, and is not my help a refuge? Am I not of your kind? Do not be concerned about your uncle's illness, for he is not going to die. Be assured, he is already well. Is there anything else you need?" Hearing and believing Mary's comforting words, Juan's heart was filled with joy. He pleaded with her to give him the sign he was to take to the bishop. Mary instructed him to climb to the top of the hill, where he would find many flowers blooming. He was to cut the flowers, gather them up, and bring them to her. Juan knew that only two days before, he had seen only rocks and a few cacti on the hill. Yet Juan believed Mary and trusted her. He climbed quickly to the top of the hill and found the most beautiful flowers he had ever seen. The frosty air was filled with a marvelous fragrance as he gathered into his mantle as many flowers as it could hold. Holding the two ends of the mantle, he returned to Mary and presented the flowers to her. Taking the flowers in her hands, she arranged them in the mantle and then, taking the two ends of the mantle from Juan's hands, tied it behind Juan's neck.

Mary said, "This is the sign that you must take to the bishop. In my name tell him that with this he will see and recognize my will and that he must do what I ask; and you, who are my ambassador worthy of my confidence, I counsel you to take every care that you open your mantle only in the presence of the bishop, and you must make it known to him what it is that you carry, and tell him how I asked you to climb to the top of the hill to gather the flowers. Tell him also all that you have seen, so that you will persuade the bishop and he will see that the church is built for which I ask." Having finished speaking, Mary said farewell to Juan.

Juan departed immediately to see the bishop. He was happy and content, and sure that this time he would succeed. Juan took great care not to injure the beautiful flowers he carried in his mantle.

When Juan arrived at the bishop's house early in the day, he met the head servant and several of his helpers and asked them to tell the bishop that he would like to see him. The servants were irritated with Juan and wouldn't let him in to see the bishop. Humbly, Juan waited outside most of the day for the servants to call him. Late in the day, the servants came out. They treated Juan roughly as they tried to see what he was carrying in his mantle. Finally, the servants told the bishop that Juan was waiting. They were surprised when the bishop told them to bring Juan to him immediately.

Juan fell to his knees before the bishop and again repeated all he had seen and heard. He told the bishop that Mary had graciously granted his request for a sign. He told about the beautiful roses on the hill, how Mary had arranged them in his mantle, and how no one was to see them before the bishop. Juan told the bishop that Mary sent the roses as the sign he had asked for, which would testify to the truth of Juan's message. With that, Juan rose to his feet, untied the mantle from behind his neck, and said, "Behold, receive them!" as the roses fell to the floor.

On Juan's mantle, where the roses had been, suddenly there appeared the Precious Image of the Immaculate Virgin, Holy Mary, Mother of God.

The bishop and all who were present fell to their knees and gazed in awe and reverence. Shedding tears of deep sorrow, the bishop prayed, begging forgiveness for not carrying out Mary's request. Rising to his feet, the bishop reverently removed from Juan Diego's neck the mantle containing the heavenly image of Mary and put it away safely in his own chapel.

Juan remained at the bishop's house for another day. The following morning, he showed the bishop where the Queen of Heaven wanted her chapel built.

Juan told the bishop he must return home to see if his uncle had been cured, as Mary had promised. Several servants accompanied Juan and, arriving at his home, found his uncle well and happy. His uncle told Juan and the others that Mary had appeared to him and cured him. Mary had told him that she had sent Juan to Mexico City to see the bishop. Mary asked Juan's uncle to tell the bishop all that he had seen and heard. He was to tell

the bishop of his miraculous cure and to request that Mary be known as the Blessed Image, the Ever Virgin, Holy Mary of Guadalupe.

Then the Spaniards and Indians, who had been enemies, worked together, building a chapel on the spot where Mary had appeared to Juan Diego. The chapel took two weeks to complete, and Juan and his uncle were guests of the bishop during this time.

Juan's mantle containing the sacred image of Mary was brought to the new chapel for all to see. (It can still be seen at the Basilica of Our Lady of Guadalupe in Mexico City.)

On a special day, all the people, Indians and Spaniards together, joined in a procession to the chapel to honor Mary. Mary had brought the people together with the miracle of Guadalupe. We celebrate the feast day of Our Lady of Guadalupe on December 12.

Saint Bernadette and Our Lady of Lourdes

LOURDES is a small town located in a valley near the Pyrenees Mountains in France. Bernadette and her family lived in Lourdes. Bernadette's family was very poor. Fourteen-year-old Bernadette, her father, mother, a sister, and two brothers lived in a small room that the townspeople nicknamed "the dungeon", because it used to be a small jail in which prisoners were held. The windows even had bars on them. Often there was not enough food to eat. Sometimes Bernadette's brother Jean-Marie was found in the local church, eating wax from melted candles. Bernadette had severe asthma and was often sick. As a result, she missed a great deal of school and had not yet received her First Communion.

One cold February morning in 1858, Bernadette, with her sister Marie-Toinette and her friend Jeanne, went outside to collect firewood. (They needed the firewood to cook their meals and warm the house.) They walked through town and didn't find much wood. They crossed a meadow and came to an area called Massabieille, where there were three large caverns in a hill. One was a grotto with an arched entrance. Bushes and moss grew on the sides of the grotto. Usually, no one went into these caverns, except to escape a storm. On the other side of a stream near the caverns, the children saw some tree limbs on the ground. Jeanne and Marie took off their shoes and quickly crossed the stream. Bernadette wanted the others to throw some big stones into the stream so that she could cross on the stones and not get her feet wet. When the other children refused, Bernadette suggested that Jeanne carry her across.

Jeanne and Marie teased Bernadette and told her to stay where she was. Then they went ahead to collect wood. Bernadette decided to look for a more shallow place to cross the stream. As she was deciding how to cross, she heard a noise, like the wind blowing. Bernadette saw a rosebush begin to glow. A Lady in a long, white gown appeared. Two roses were on her feet, and she carried a rosary. Bernadette knelt down and took out the rosary that was in her pocket. Bernadette said the Rosary, and then the Lady disappeared. When Jeanne and Marie came back, they found Bernadette kneeling. The girls began to tease her again. "Are you ever lazy! Wait until Sunday to pray!"

Bernadette ignored the teasing. She asked the girls whether they had seen anything. They said they hadn't, so Bernadette told them what she had seen. The girls told Bernadette that if she continued to tell stories like that, everyone in town would make fun of her. Bernadette decided not to say anything more about the Lady.

However, Marie and Jeanne did tell others. Bernadette's mother, Louise, was angry. She thought that either Bernadette was making up the story or the devil was playing tricks on her. She would not allow Bernadette to go back to the grotto.

One Sunday, Bernadette, Marie, and some friends persuaded Bernadette's parents to allow her to go to the grotto. One of them brought along some holy water, which they would use to send away the devil, if he appeared.

When they arrived at the grotto, Bernadette told the girls to pray the Rosary. "Look, there she is", whispered Bernadette. She took the holy water and sprinkled some of it toward the Lady she saw.

The girls saw that Bernadette looked very happy, but they could not see anything special. Bernadette's eyes were wide open, looking at the grotto. Her friends tried to get her to talk, but Bernadette didn't respond. The friends became afraid. They ran to get some help. A nearby miller and his mother walked Bernadette back to their house. On the way there, Bernadette's eyes kept staring at something above her.

Once they arrived at the house, Bernadette could no longer see the vision. She excitedly told everyone that she had seen the lovely Lady with the rosary again.

Word spread quickly throughout the small town of Lourdes. Soon, Bernadette's mother came to the miller's house. She was afraid that the family would become the laughing-stock of the town. She forbade Bernadette to go to the grotto again.

Bernadette was afraid the Lady would forget her. However, two women from town talked Bernadette's mother into letting the girl go with them to the grotto. Bernadette ran ahead of the two women; her asthma was not bothering her. When the women reached the grotto, they saw Bernadette kneeling and praying the Rosary.

Suddenly, Bernadette cried, "She's there!" Even though the women could not see anything special, they knelt down and prayed the Rosary with Bernadette. When they had finished, one of the women said, "Ask the Lady what she wants. Have her write it down." Bernadette took the paper the woman gave her. But when she gave the paper back to the women, it was still blank.

The women asked why the paper was still blank. Bernadette said, "The Lady said it was not necessary to write everything down. Then she told me that she could not promise me happiness in this world, but in the next. The Lady asked me to keep coming here every day for two weeks." Bernadette was astonished that the women had not heard the Lady. Bernadette had heard her so clearly.

The two women believed what Bernadette had told them and quickly spread the story throughout Lourdes. When Bernadette arrived home, she

The stained glass image shows Mary with text in her halo reading "I AM THE IMMACULATE CONCEPTION"

told her parents what she had seen and heard. They decided that Bernadette could go to the grotto the next day, and her mother decided to go with her.

This time, when Bernadette arrived at the grotto, many people, drawn by curiosity, were already there. Bernadette knelt down and began to pray the Rosary. As she prayed, a radiant smile appeared on her face. The others present had never seen anyone glow with such happiness or look so beautiful. About half an hour later, Bernadette seemed to "wake up". Her mother asked if the Lady had said anything. Bernadette said that the Lady would make revelations to her.

The next day, the police took Bernadette in for questioning. The police chief tried to get Bernadette to say that she had made up the story. But Bernadette would not, because she had not lied. Bernadette was released when her father promised that he would not allow her to return to the grotto.

Bernadette was glad to be home, but she was worried. She knew she would have to choose whether to disobey her parents and go to the grotto as the Lady requested, or to disobey the Lady.

The next day, a Monday, Bernadette was given strict instructions: "Go directly to religion class and nowhere else." When she arrived at school, the younger children teased her. When her teacher asked her to recite some prayers from memory, Bernadette was unable to say them. At lunchtime, Bernadette walked slowly home. She wanted to go to the grotto. After lunch, she headed back to school. Suddenly, she turned and ran to the grotto. Children playing in a field saw her run past, and they yelled out, "Bernadette's going to Massabieille." Soon, a crowd followed her. Even the police came. Bernadette waited and waited, but the Lady did not appear. Bernadette walked sadly home. The townspeople joked that the Lady was afraid of the police.

The teasing did not stop Bernadette. On Tuesday, after morning Mass, Bernadette went back to the grotto. There were already a couple of hundred people there. Bernadette took her rosary in her hands, knelt down, and began to pray. As she finished the first decade, a beautiful smile spread across her face. No one else could see what she saw. But Bernadette looked so radiant, there was no doubt that she was listening to the Lady in a vision.

On Wednesday, Bernadette saw the Lady again. The police and the town doctor watched Bernadette, and they quizzed her afterward. They were unable to prove that she was lying about the visions.

On Thursday, it was cold and rainy, yet four hundred people went to the grotto to observe Bernadette. She knelt down, and again her face filled with joy. Then, unexpectedly, she got up and moved toward the grotto. Then she bent down and dug a small hole in the ground with her hands. A little muddy water appeared. Three times Bernadette scooped out the muddy water. Finally the water was clear enough to drink. Next, she got up and walked home. The parish priest stopped Bernadette and asked her why she had done those things. Bernadette answered, "I only did what the Lady asked me to do."

Later in the day, the hole that Bernadette had dug overflowed with water. The water trickled down the stones near the grotto and created a stream that flowed toward the river. That night a stonecutter who was nearly blind sent his daughter to get some of the water. He believe it was sent by the Blessed Virgin. When he rubbed some of the water on his eyes, he was cured! He could see again! His doctor could not explain how the man recovered his sight.

Bernadette continued to visit the grotto each day. The crowds there grew larger and larger and were a worry to the police, but everyone was orderly. Some of the priests who had heard of the visions were also nervous, for they were not sure that Bernadette was seeing the Blessed Mother.

On the following Tuesday, the Lady asked Bernadette to visit the parish priest. Bernadette was afraid of him, but she went and told him: "Father, the Lady wants a chapel to be built. She also wants processions to the grotto." The priest answered: "You haven't told me the Lady's name. Go back and tell her we want her name, and we want to see a miracle."

Bernadette visited the grotto whenever possible, but the Lady did not tell Bernadette her name. Meanwhile, there were many reports of sick people being cured after touching the water in the grotto. Thousands of people visited the grotto every day, hoping to be cured or to see Bernadette's vision.

On Thursday, March 25, Bernadette again walked to the grotto. When she arrived, she saw the grotto already glowing and the Lady waiting for her. Thousands of people saw Bernadette kneel and begin to pray the Rosary. The radiant smile appeared on her face. Bernadette asked the Lady who she was. This time the Lady answered and then slowly departed.

Bernadette walked to the parish priest's house and told him: "I asked the Lady what her name was. The Lady said, 'I am the Immaculate Conception.' What does this mean?" The priest answered, "It means that Mary was conceived without sin. She has always been free of original sin." The priest asked Bernadette if she was sure that the Lady had said she was the Immaculate Conception.

"Yes", she said. "The Lady said, 'I am the Immaculate Conception.'"

When this information became known, people came night and day to the grotto. Bernadette visited the grotto each day to pray. One day, as she was holding a candle, she held her hand to protect the flame from the wind. A strong gust blew the flame into her hand, but Bernadette didn't seem to notice. When a doctor examined her hand afterward, he could not find any burn mark.

The police wanted to stop all the people from visiting the grotto. They declared that it was against the law for anyone to visit the grotto. They had a fence put up, but it did not keep people away. The police also said that anyone claiming to have seen visions would be arrested. The mayor decided he had to carry out this order. However, the parish priest told the mayor that the police would be able to arrest Bernadette only if they killed him first. The police decided not to arrest Bernadette.

During this time, many people claimed to have been healed. Henri, a fifteen-year-old boy, had a chronic sore on his throat. Henri washed his sore with water from the grotto, and the next morning the sore was gone. A young child who was completely paralyzed was also cured by the water. A woman named Catherine had a deformed hand. After Catherine dipped her hand in the water from the grotto, her hand returned to normal. The doctors who examined these people could not explain how they were cured.

On July 16, the feast day of Our Lady of Mount Carmel, Bernadette went to church to pray. She heard a quiet voice telling her to go to the grotto. Bernadette went to the grotto and knelt down. She trembled with joy. The Blessed Mother smiled at Bernadette and disappeared. This was the eighteenth time Bernadette had seen her. She never saw her again.

A bishop who questioned Bernadette was convinced that she was telling the truth about her visions. He said he would order a commission to study what had happened at the grotto.

On October 5, the emperor of France declared that from that day on, everyone would be allowed to enter the grotto freely, without any fear of arrest.

When Bernadette was sixteen, the bishop declared that life at home was too hard for Bernadette. She went to live in a hospice, helping the Sisters there by working in the kitchen and in the hospital. Bernadette was often very sick with her asthma. But when the Sisters asked her to give interviews, she never refused, even though she disliked doing so.

When Bernadette was eighteen, the commission that the bishop had formed to investigate her visions finally reached a decision. They decided that the Mother of God had appeared to Bernadette eighteen times. The bishop then asked all the bishops in France to help build a chapel on the site of the visions.

Bernadette wanted peace and quiet, in order to have time to pray. At the age of twenty-one, she decided to enter the convent of the Sisters of Charity and Christian Instruction of Nevers. She took the name Sister Marie Bernard. When she arrived at the convent, the Sisters had already been told by their Mother Superior that Bernadette would talk to them about her experience the following evening, that they could ask her questions, but that afterward they were not to bring up the subject again.

Bernadette spent much of her time praying. She tried to work hard, even though she was often sick. In fact, she became even more sick. Sores appeared on her leg and brought her severe pain, but she never complained about it.

When she was only thirty-six years old, in 1876, Bernadette died. Her body has since been enclosed in a glass case. Today, more that a hundred years later, her body shows no sign of decay. In fact, she is as beautiful now as she was when she died. In 1925, Bernadette was declared a saint.

Many people visit Lourdes today. Many people are still being cured there, and many of these cures are considered miracles.

Unit 6

Liturgical
Seasons

20

Advent: Preparing for Jesus' Birthday

CONCEPTS OF FAITH

What is Advent?
Advent is the season before Christmas. During Advent we prepare for the celebration of Jesus' birthday.

What is Christmas?
Christmas is the day we celebrate Jesus' birthday.

Have you understood the lessons of the shepherds? They listen to the voice of the angel, set out in search of Him at once and finally find Jesus. We all must look for Jesus. Very often we must look for Him because we do not know Him yet; at other times because we have lost Him; and at other times, we look for Him in order to know Him better, to love Him more and to make Him loved.

POPE JOHN PAUL II

A Time of Preparation

Advent is the season before Christmas. Advent includes four Sundays. During Advent we want to spend time preparing ourselves for Jesus' birthday. We think about Jesus and what He has done for us. We think about ways that we can change so that we can be more like Jesus.

For example, maybe we have not loved God and others as Jesus taught us. We think about how we can change in order to be closer to Jesus. We can prepare for Jesus' birthday by doing special things for our families and friends and by trying to act more like Jesus.

The Christmas Story

Leader: God the Father promised that He would send a Savior. God the Son is our Savior. Jesus shows us who we are and how we should act as images of God. Jesus returned God's love and He helps us return God's love. Jesus is the Light of the world.

The Advent wreath is circular. A circle has no beginning and has no end. The circle reminds us that God always was and always will be. The evergreen branches used in our Advent wreath remind us that God never changes and that He always loves us. The four candles represent the four Sundays of Advent, during which we prepare for Jesus' birthday. When we light these candles, we remember that Jesus is the Light of the world. He brings us hope, peace, joy, and love.

I. *The First Candle*

Leader: The prophet Isaiah wrote: "Therefore the Lord himself will give you this sign: the virgin shall be with child, and bear a son, and shall name him Immanuel" (Isaiah 7:14).

Reader 1: The first candle reminds us of hope.
[*Light the first candle on the Advent wreath.*]

Reader 2: The Annunciation. (based on Luke 1:26–56)
When Mary was a young girl, she became engaged to Joseph. God sent the angel Gabriel to Mary. Gabriel said, "Hail, favored one! The Lord is with you." Mary did not understand. Gabriel told her not to be afraid. He explained that the Lord had blessed her. God had chosen her to be the Mother of His Son. Mary wondered how this could happen. Gabriel told her that the Holy Spirit would come to her. Nothing was impossible with God. Mary answered that she was the Lord's servant and would do as He asked. Mary trusted in God. She had hope.

Reader 3: Later, Mary went to visit her cousin Elizabeth, who was expecting a baby. When Elizabeth saw Mary, she was filled with joy from God. Elizabeth cried out, "Most blessed are you among women, and blessed is the fruit of your womb." Mary responded, "My soul proclaims the greatness of the Lord; my spirit rejoices in God my savior." She said that God had kept His promises.

Leader: Like Mary, we have hope. We have hope that we can become better friends with Jesus.

All: Come, Lord Jesus, and light our way with hope.

II. *The Second Candle*

Leader: The prophet Isaiah wrote: "The wolf shall be a guest of the lamb, and the leopard shall lie down with the kid; the calf and the young lion shall browse together, with a little child to guide them" (Isaiah 11:6).

Reader 1: The second candle reminds us of peace.
[*Light the second candle in the Advent wreath.*]

Reader 2: Jesus, the Prince of Peace, Is Born.   (based on Luke 2:1–7)
After Joseph and Mary were married, a ruler named Caesar Augustus wanted to know how many people he ruled. Caesar Augustus ordered all people to go back to their hometowns to be counted. Mary and Joseph had to travel to Bethlehem. It was a long journey from Nazareth to Bethlehem. When they arrived in Bethlehem, it was time for Mary's baby to be born. Bethlehem was very crowded, and there was no room in any of the inns for them. They found shelter in a nearby stable. There Jesus was born. Mary wrapped Jesus in swaddling clothes and laid him in a manger.

Leader: Jesus acted as a peacemaker. Let us take a few moments and think about how we can be peacemakers. [*Pause.*]

All: Come, Lord Jesus, and light our way with peace.

III. *The Third Candle*

Leader: The prophet Isaiah wrote: "The people who walked in darkness have seen a great light; upon those who dwelt in the land of gloom a light has shone. You have brought them abundant joy and great rejoicing . . ." (Isaiah 9:1–2).

Reader 1: The third candle reminds us of joy.
[*Light the third candle on the Advent wreath.*]

Reader 2: The Shepherds Come to See Jesus.   (based on Luke 2:8–20) There were shepherds in a nearby field watching their sheep. Suddenly the sky was filled with a bright light, and the shepherds became afraid. The shepherds looked up in the sky and saw many angels. An angel told the shepherds not to be afraid. The angel had good news for the shepherds. He told them that a Savior had been born in Bethlehem. The shepherds could find Him in a manger, wrapped in swaddling clothes. Then the angels began to praise God. "Glory to God in the highest and on earth peace to those on whom his favor rests."

Reader 3: When the angels returned to heaven, the shepherds began to talk to one another. They decided to go to Bethlehem and visit the baby Jesus. The shepherds found Mary and Joseph in the stable. Lying in the manger, wrapped in swaddling clothes, was Jesus. The shepherds explained that the angels

had told them about Jesus' birth. The shepherds began to praise God. Mary listened to everything they said and kept those things in her heart.

When the shepherds left, they told everyone what they had seen and what they had been told.

Leader: There was great joy when Jesus was born. Let us thank Jesus for being our Savior. We know that if we follow Jesus, we will someday live in heaven with Him.

All: Come, Lord Jesus, and light our way with joy.

IV. *The Fourth Candle*

Leader: The prophet Isaiah wrote: "For a child is born to us, a son is given us; upon his shoulder dominion rests. They name him Wonder-Counselor, God-Hero, Father-Forever, Prince of Peace" (Isaiah 9:5).

Reader 1: The fourth candle reminds us of love.
[*Light the fourth candle on the Advent wreath.*]

Reader 2: The Wise Men Visit Jesus.   (based on Matthew 2:1–12)
Sometime after Jesus was born, Wise Men arrived in Jerusalem. They had been following a bright star. They stopped at King Herod's to ask him for help. They asked, "Where is the newborn king of the Jews?" The Wise Men explained that they had seen His star rise and had come to praise Him. King Herod was worried. He called all of his advisors. He asked them if they knew what the Wise Men were talking about. His advisors explained that, long ago, a prophet had written that in Bethlehem a king would come who would be a leader of the Israelite people. King Herod

went back to the Wise Men. He told them that the Child could be found in Bethlehem. King Herod told the Wise Men to go and find Him. King Herod then wanted them to return and tell him about what they had found, so he could honor the Child also.

Reader 3: The Wise Men followed the star again. They followed this bright star until it stopped. The star stopped above the place where Jesus was. The Wise Men went inside and saw Mary and Jesus. They knelt before Jesus and praised Him. The Wise Men gave Jesus gifts of frankincense, gold, and myrrh. Afterward, the Wise Men were warned in a dream not to return to King Herod. So they returned to their country using a different route.

Leader: On Christmas Day we celebrate God's greatest gift to us, Jesus. We celebrate the love God has for us, and the love we have for God and others. We usually give family members and friends presents on their birthdays. We do this because we love and care for them. On Christmas, we want to share our love for Jesus and for each other. We can't give Jesus frankincense, gold, and myrrh as the Wise Men did. But we know Jesus loves each of us, so we give each other presents. This is a sign of our love for Jesus and for each other. We can help bring Jesus' love to other people by trying to act like Him.

All: Come, Lord Jesus, and light our way with love.

These are ways I can prepare myself for Jesus' birthday, Christmas.

21

Lent:
The Path to New Life

What is Lent?
Lent is the time when we prepare ourselves for the joy and new life of Easter.

When does Lent begin?
On Ash Wednesday.

What kind of good works and penances can we practice during Lent?
Fasting and abstinence, prayer, charity toward our neighbor.

On what day does Holy Week begin?
Palm Sunday.

What days make up the Easter Triduum?
Holy Thursday, Good Friday, Holy Saturday, and Easter Sunday.

What events do we celebrate on the days of the Easter Triduum?
The Last Supper, Jesus' Passion and death, Jesus' Resurrection.

Vocabulary

abstinence: to go without something completely.
infirmities: weaknesses.

> *Jesus, our Brother, took our place in order to make up for sin. To do so He had to suffer the passion and death on the cross.*
>
> *Lent is the path towards the joy of the meeting with the risen Christ.*
>
> POPE JOHN PAUL II

Sharing the Sacrifice of Jesus

Lent begins with Ash Wednesday and ends on Holy Thursday. During the Mass on Ash Wednesday, a priest, deacon, or Eucharistic minister traces the shape of a cross with ashes on your forehead.

The ashes are a sign of dust. As the ashes are put on our foreheads, we are reminded that God made us from nothing and that someday we will die. We are called to be sorry for our sins and to do penance. We are called to be faithful to Jesus.

> *Fasting means putting a limit on so many desires, sometimes good ones, in order to have full control of oneself, to learn to control one's own feelings, to train the will in good.*
> —Pope John Paul II

Saint John the Baptist told the people of his time, "Repent, for the kingdom of heaven is at hand!" (Matthew 3:2). John asked the people to change their lives and to love and obey God.

Lent is a time when we should look into our hearts and look at the choices we have made in our lives. Sometimes, we don't love as we should, and we make wrong choices. We should be sorry for our sins, and we should ask God to forgive us in the sacrament of Reconciliation.

We should use the time of Lent to grow in our love for God. We can grow in our love for God by practicing good works and some form of penance. Some of the good works and penances we can practice are: fasting and abstinence, prayer, and charity toward our neighbor.

Fasting. Fasting is choosing to do less often something we enjoy doing. When we eat less food at meals or go without candy, we are fasting. We are also fasting when we watch less TV or give up watching our favorite TV program. We can make our fasting a sacrifice done out of love for God.

Abstinence. Going without something completely is abstinence. As Catholics, we abstain from eating meat on Ash Wednesday and on every Friday during Lent.

Prayer. We should pray every day, of course. But during Lent, we should make an effort to pray more often each day. For example, if we watch less TV during Lent, we can use the time to pray instead. We should especially call to mind Jesus' Passion and death. We can increase the time we spend in prayer by going to Mass daily, by praying the Sorrowful Mysteries of the Rosary, and by going to the Stations of the Cross.

Charity toward Our Neighbor. Charity is another word for love. Charity toward our neighbor means that we should be loving and kind toward other people—our families, our friends, our neighbors, and, in fact, all people. We should treat them with love and respect, we should pray for them, we should share what we have with them, and we should help them when we are able to do so. The theological virtue of charity helps us to be loving and kind toward others.

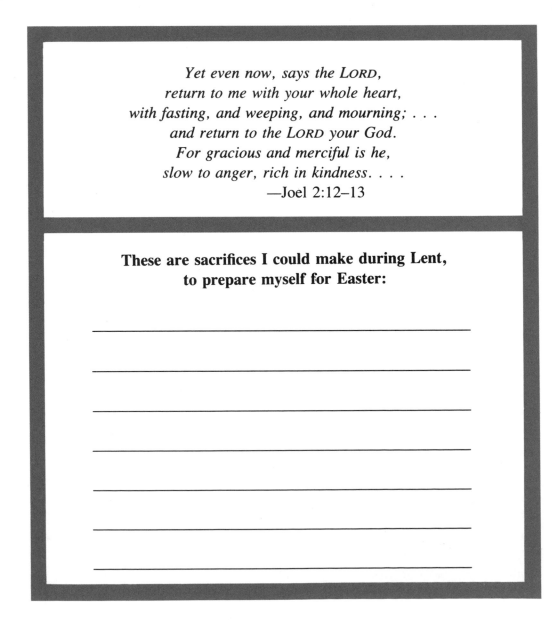

Yet even now, says the LORD,
return to me with your whole heart,
with fasting, and weeping, and mourning; . . .
and return to the LORD your God.
For gracious and merciful is he,
slow to anger, rich in kindness. . . .
—Joel 2:12–13

These are sacrifices I could make during Lent,
to prepare myself for Easter:

_____

_____

_____

_____

_____

_____

_____

Hosanna to the Son of David; blessed is he who comes in the name of the Lord; hosanna in the highest.
    —Matthew 21:9

Jesus' Entry into Jerusalem

Jesus and his disciples were on their way to Jerusalem to celebrate the feast of Passover. When they reached the place called the Mount of Olives, Jesus sent two of His disciples into a village nearby. Jesus told them to untie the donkey they would find there and to bring it to Him. If the owner questioned them, the disciples were to tell him that Jesus needed it and the owner would send it at once. The two disciples went and did as Jesus had told them. They brought the donkey to Jesus. They laid their cloaks on the donkey and helped Jesus climb onto its back. As Jesus started down from the Mount of Olives into Jerusalem, a very large crowd of people welcomed Him. They waved palm branches in the air and laid their cloaks and palm branches on the road ahead of Him. They rejoiced and praised God, saying: "Hosanna to the Son of David; blessed is he who comes in the name of the Lord; hosanna in the highest."

There were some Pharisees in the crowd who told Jesus to stop the people from saying these things. Jesus told the Pharisees that, even if the people were silent, the very stones would shout. Then Jesus went into the temple to teach the people.

On Palm Sunday, we celebrate Jesus' entry into Jerusalem, and we remember the crowd of people waving palm branches and praising Jesus as their king.

    —based on Matthew 21:1–17, Luke 19:28–40

The Easter Triduum

During the Easter Triduum, we celebrate Jesus' Passion, death, and Resurrection. The Easter Triduum begins on Holy Thursday evening. On Holy Thursday the Church re-presents the Last Supper that Jesus shared with His Apostles. At the Last Supper, Jesus gave us the sacraments of the Holy Eucharist and Holy Orders.

"Take and eat; this is my body. . . . Drink from it, all of you, for this is my blood of the covenant, which will be shed on behalf of many for the forgiveness of sins."
—Matthew 26:26–28

The Lord's Supper

Jesus and His Apostles went to Jerusalem to celebrate Passover. They gathered in a room for the Passover. There, Jesus washed the feet of the Apostles. He did this to show them that they should love and serve each other and all people.

Jesus took the unleavened bread, blessed it, and broke it. He gave it to His Apostles and said to them, "Take and eat; this is my body." Then Jesus took a cup of wine and gave thanks. Jesus gave the cup to the Apostles and said, "Drink from it, all of you, for this is my blood of the covenant, which will be shed on behalf of many for the forgiveness of sins."

Then Jesus and the Apostles went to the Garden of Gethsemane, where Jesus, in great sorrow, prayed to God the Father.
—based on John 13, Matthew 26:26–46

Yet it was our infirmities that he bore, our sufferings that he endured, . . . But he was pierced for our offenses, crushed for our sins. Upon him was the chastisement that makes us whole, by his stripes we were healed.
—Isaiah 53:4–5

Because he surrendered himself to death . . . he shall take away the sins of many, and win pardon for their offenses.
—Isaiah 53:12

Good Friday

On Good Friday, we remember Jesus' suffering and death. Jesus suffered and died for us, because of His great love for us.

During the Good Friday liturgy, we can receive Holy Communion, and we can honor the crucifix. One way we can especially remember Jesus' suffering and death is by making the Stations of the Cross.

Stations of the Cross

Jesus has been scourged [whipped], and a crown of thorns has been placed on His head. His poor body is covered with bleeding wounds.

The First Station: *Jesus Is Condemned to Death*
In this station, we remember that Pontius Pilate condemned Jesus to death on the Cross. Jesus knew that God the Father wanted Him to accept death on the Cross as a sacrifice of love. We should ask Jesus to help us obey our parents, even when it is hard for us.

The Second Station: *Jesus Takes His Cross*
In this station, we remember that Jesus must have been tired and in pain after being whipped and made to wear a crown of thorns. Then the soldiers gave Jesus a heavy cross to carry to the place where He would be crucified. This station reminds us not to complain but to ask Jesus to help us accept our own crosses.

The Third Station: *Jesus Falls the First Time*
In this station, we remember how Jesus, tired from His beatings, falls down for the first time. Jesus gets back up, picks up His Cross, and continues His journey. We should ask Jesus to help us when we are tired and tempted to quit before we complete our work.

The Fourth Station: *Jesus Meets His Mother*
In this station, we remember when Jesus meets His Mother, Mary. As Jesus carries the heavy Cross, He looks up and sees Mary. Mary loves Jesus so much, and she shares in His sorrow and suffering. We should ask Jesus to help us love Mary, our heavenly Mother.

The Fifth Station: *Jesus Is Helped by Simon*
In this station, we remember when the soldiers, knowing that Jesus was very tired, made Simon of Cyrene help Jesus carry the Cross. We should ask Jesus to help us admit when we need help.

The Sixth Station: *Veronica Wipes Jesus' Face*
In this station, we remember Veronica's compassion as she wipes the blood and sweat from Jesus' face. We should ask Jesus to make us aware of people who need our help and to inspire us to help them.

The Seventh Station: *Jesus Falls a Second Time*
In this station, we remember how Jesus falls a second time and somehow finds the strength to get up and continue walking. We should ask Jesus to help us keep trying to make right choices, even though sometimes we fail.

The Eighth Station: *Jesus Meets the Women*
In this station, we remember how Jesus meets a group of women who are His friends. They are very sad, and they are weeping. They don't understand why Jesus is going to die. We should ask Jesus to help us and guide us when we don't understand why certain things happen.

The Ninth Station: *Jesus Falls a Third Time*
In this station, we remember Jesus falling a third time. It is harder for Him to stand up this time. We should be sorry for making the same wrong choice again and again. We should ask Jesus to forgive us and to help us do better.

The Tenth Station: *Jesus Is Stripped of His Clothes*
In this station, we remember how the soldiers took off Jesus' clothes so roughly that the wounds on His back were reopened. The people make fun of Him for not saving Himself. We should ask Jesus to help us not become angry when others make fun of us while we are trying to do what is right.

The Eleventh Station: *Jesus Is Nailed to the Cross*
In this station, we remember how the soldiers nailed Jesus' hands and feet to the Cross. We should remember how much Jesus loves us.

The Twelfth Station: *Jesus Dies*
In this station, we remember how Jesus hung on the Cross for three hours and then died for us. We should decide to do small sacrifices to show our love for Jesus.

The Thirteenth Station: *Jesus Is Taken Down from the Cross*
In this station, we remember how Jesus was taken down from the Cross and laid in Mary's arms. We should ask Jesus to help us comfort those who are sad and lonely.

The Fourteenth Station: *Jesus Is Buried in a Tomb*
In this station, we remember how Jesus' body was wrapped in a clean linen cloth and laid in a new tomb. We should ask Jesus to help us be more like Him. We should also remember to pray for those who have died.

If then you were raised with Christ, seek what is above, where Christ is seated at the right hand of God. Think of what is above, not of what is on earth.
—Colossians 3:1–2

The Easter Vigil

The Easter Triduum continues with the Easter Vigil Mass on Holy Saturday evening. On this night the Church celebrates the Resurrection of Jesus. During the Easter Vigil, fire is blessed and the Paschal candle is lighted, reminding us that Jesus is the light of the world. The readings and Gospel are read. Water is blessed. This blessed water is sometimes used for baptisms at the Easter Vigil Mass.

The Resurrection of Jesus

At daybreak, Mary Magdalene, Joanna, and Mary the mother of James went to the tomb where Jesus had been buried. They took with them some spices they had prepared.

When they arrived at the tomb, they found the stone rolled away from the entrance. The women entered the tomb, but they didn't find the body of Jesus. The women were very puzzled. Suddenly, two men dressed in dazzling white appeared to them. The women were afraid. The men said, "Why do you seek the living one among the dead? He is not here, but he has been raised. Remember what he said to you while he was still in Galilee, that the Son of Man must be handed over to sinners and be crucified, and rise on the third day."

The women remembered Jesus' words. The women told the Apostles all the things they had seen and heard.

—based on Luke 24

Jesus said,

"So be perfect, just as your heavenly Father is perfect."
(Matthew 5:48)

Jesus is asking us to be loving, kind, and forgiving.
One way we can work at being loving, kind, and forgiving
is by practicing the virtues.

Practicing the virtues will help us to be
the best images of God we can be.

The virtue I will practice during Lent is:

_____

This virtue helps me to:

_____

_____

_____

Name: _____

Date: _____

Prayers to Know

Our Father

Our Father, Who art in heaven,
hallowed be Thy name;
Thy kingdom come;
Thy will be done on earth as it is in heaven.
Give us this day our daily bread;
and forgive us our trespasses as we forgive those who trespass against us;
and lead us not into temptation, but deliver us from evil.
Amen.

Apostles' Creed

I believe in God, the Father almighty,
   Creator of heaven and earth.
I believe in Jesus Christ, His only Son, our Lord.
   He was conceived by the power of the Holy Spirit
      and born of the Virgin Mary.
   He suffered under Pontius Pilate,
      was crucified, died, and was buried.
   He descended to the dead.
   On the third day He rose again.
   He ascended into heaven,
      and is seated at the right hand of the Father.
   He will come again to judge the living and the dead.
I believe in the Holy Spirit,
   the holy Catholic Church,
   the communion of saints,
   the forgiveness of sins,
   the resurrection of the body,
   and the life everlasting.
Amen.

Glory Be

Glory be to the Father, and to the Son, and to the Holy Spirit,
as it was in the beginning, is now, and ever shall be, world without end.
Amen.

Hail Mary

Hail, Mary, full of grace, the Lord is with thee.
Blessed art thou among women, and blessed is the fruit of thy womb, Jesus.
Holy Mary, Mother of God,
pray for us sinners now and at the hour of our death.
Amen.

Hail, Holy Queen

Hail, holy Queen, Mother of mercy,
    our life, our sweetness and our hope.
To you do we cry, poor banished children of Eve.
To you do we send up our sighs,
    mourning and weeping in this vale of tears.
Turn then, most gracious advocate,
    your eyes of mercy toward us,
    and after this exile
    show to us the blessed fruit of your womb, Jesus.
O clement, O loving, O sweet Virgin Mary.
    V. Pray for us, O holy Mother of God.
    R. That we may be made worthy of the promises of Christ.

Angelus

The angel of the Lord declared unto Mary:
And she conceived by the Holy Spirit.
    Hail, Mary, . . .
Behold the handmaid of the Lord:
Be it done to me according to Your word.
    Hail, Mary, . . .
And the Word was made flesh:
And dwelt among us.
    Hail, Mary, . . .
Pray for us, O holy Mother of God:
That we may be made worthy of the promises of Christ.
    Pour forth, we beseech You, O Lord, Your grace into our hearts, that we
    to whom the Incarnation of Christ, Your Son, was made known by the
    message of an angel, may by His Passion and Cross be brought to the
    glory of His resurrection. Through Christ our Lord. Amen.

Memorare

Remember, O most gracious Virgin Mary,
  that never was it known
  that anyone who fled to your protection,
  implored your help,
  or sought your intercession,
  was left unaided.
Inspired by this confidence,
  I fly unto you, O Virgin of virgins, my Mother.
To you do I come, before you I stand, sinful and sorrowful.
O Mother of the Word Incarnate,
  despise not my petitions,
  but in your mercy hear and answer me.
Amen.

Act of Contrition

My God,
I am sorry for my sins with all my heart.
In choosing to do wrong and failing to do good,
I have sinned against You,
  Whom I should love above all things.
I have hurt myself and others.
I firmly intend, with Your help,
  to do penance, to sin no more,
  and to avoid whatever leads me to sin.
Our Savior Jesus Christ suffered and died for us.
In His name, my God, have mercy.
Amen.

Morning Offering

O Jesus, through the Immaculate Heart of Mary,
I offer You my prayers, works, joys, and sufferings of this day
in union with the Holy Sacrifice of the Mass throughout the world.
I offer them for all the intentions of Your Sacred Heart:
the salvation of souls,
reparation for sin,
the reunion of all Christians.
I offer them for the intentions of our bishops
and of all Apostles of Prayer,
and in particular for those recommended by our Holy Father this month.
Amen.

—Apostleship of Prayer

Grace before Meals

Bless us, O Lord, and these Thy gifts,
which we are about to receive from Thy bounty.
Through Christ our Lord.
Amen.

Grace after Meals

We give Thee thanks for all Thy gifts, almighty God.
You live and reign forever.
Amen.

An Act of Faith

O my God, I firmly believe that You are one God in three Divine Persons,
    Father, Son, and Holy Spirit.
I believe that Your Divine Son became man and died for our sins,
    and that He will come to judge the living and the dead.
I believe these and all the truths which the holy Catholic Church teaches,
    because You have revealed them, Who can neither deceive nor be deceived.
Amen.

An Act of Hope

O my God, relying on Your infinite goodness and promises,
    I hope to obtain pardon of my sins,
    the help of Your grace,
    and life everlasting,
    through the merits of Jesus Christ,
        my Lord and Redeemer.
Amen.

An Act of Love

O my God, I love You above all things,
    with my whole heart and soul,
    because You are all-good and worthy of all my love.
I love my neighbor as myself for the love of You.
I forgive all who have injured me,
    and ask pardon of all whom I have injured.
Amen.

NOTES

NOTES

NOTES

NOTES